How to Make Things Go Your Way

Ralph Charell

FRANKLIN WATTS
New York/London/Toronto
1979

*With gratitude and thanks to
many wonderful people for being there
when it made all the difference.
There is no way to repay this debt except,
perhaps, by passing it on to others.*

R.C.

Lyrics from *American Pie* by Don McLean
copyright © 1971 Mayday Music and Yahweh Tunes, Inc.
Used by permission.

Library of Congress Cataloging in Publication Data

Charell, Ralph.
How to make things go your way.

1.   Success.   I.   Title.
BF637.S8C445   158′.1   79-14484
ISBN 0-531-09911-3

Contents

Once Upon a Time
1

Personal Relationships
15

Communication
30

Not Even Superman Works Alone
45

Looking Good
59

Playfulness
75

Feeling Great
87

Working
102

Dealing
119

Making Things Happen
134

Calling Your Own Plays;
Playing Your Own Calls
148

Bread: The Big Loaf
161

Spirit
178

How to Make
Things Go
Your Way

And I knew if I had my chance
That I could make those people dance
And maybe they'd be happy for a while.

Don McLean
American Pie

Once Upon a Time

Once upon a time, so long ago we can hardly remember it now, each of us had a dream of what life would be like. I suppose all I ever really wanted out of life was to be myself, to feel at home in the world, and to do well by doing good. Although others might express their hopes and dreams differently, if they were to go back far enough in their memories (to when all the people they knew were still the "good guys"), I think most would admit they wanted much the same. But circumstances beyond our control got in the way (or so we thought), and here we are now.

We have all faced our own forks in the road. In my case, after stumbling into the securities business when I got out of law school, I'd worked my way from order clerk to president of a firm on Wall Street that bore my name. From that position, I had the time and the perspective to discover that the world of stocks and bonds was not where I wanted to spend the rest of my career years. I began to write comedy material. We were entering the turbulent sixties. Against the backdrop of the Cuban Missile Crisis, our deepening involvement in Vietnam, civil rights marches, and the assassination of our president, I was trying to discover who I was and how I could help. I had the crazy notion I had something to say and that I could somehow become "a force for good." On the few occasions I was brash enough to disclose this intention to more than one person at a time, they would look at one another sidewise for a long moment and make no reply.

Persistence, imagination, and the flexibility to accept a job I really didn't want (but one within the field of communications) enabled me to leap the chasm into the broadcasting industry. I was on another ladder and climbing. In the summer of 1973, married and with a daughter coming of college age, I resigned from my post as a network television program executive, with no other gig in sight and no clear picture of where I was going. I'd been with the network almost nine years, had a law degree and a bachelor's degree, as well as a Master of Fine Arts in film, television, and radio, and thought of myself as an extremely capable, even gifted, communicator. But I wasn't in charge of my area of responsibility and had little political and social leverage within the company for getting my ideas and projects onto the home screen. I had outgrown my terrarium but repeated requests for replanting had produced only promises.

It was ill-advised to resign without planning the next move in advance and the timing was way off, but there was a growing sense of a clear choice between facing the uncertainties of making my way from where I was to where I wanted to be, and the prospect of being submerged into a loss of my own persona. After a brief discussion with my family in which I explained my perceptions of the choice I faced, and the uncertainties for us inherent in the course I wanted to take (which couldn't have been reassuring), I cut myself adrift.

Several months later, my first book, *How I Turn Ordinary Complaints into Thousands of Dollars*, was published, and it was extremely well received. People throughout the land were "mad as hell and not going to take it anymore." As the person recognized by the *Guinness Book of World Records* as "the world's most successful complainer," I certainly knew the feeling. The book tapped directly into the mood of the country, was an almost immediate top-ten national best seller, and was praised by reviewers far beyond my expectations.

I'd learned to beat the system at its own game and was now showing others how to do so. In efforts to correct certain abuses of the marketplace that would occasionally overtake some of my innocent pursuits, I'd gone up against giant corporations, worldwide conglomerates, doctors, lawyers, bankers, brokers, airlines, department stores, restaurants, public utilities, and others, singlehandedly, armed only with my own wits and nerve, a sense of right and wrong and a modicum of rage and outrage. With only a couple of minor exceptions, my track record was perfect, and I could have gone on being the world's most successful complainer for decades.

The role I had fallen into and subsequently accepted had me cast as a kind of "public conscience." It wasn't bad and it had its built-in rewards. I had hundreds of interviews in the media. Scores of feature stories in the press were extremely complimentary. My other books made national best seller lists, and the Mark Twain Society knighted me for my "outstanding contribution to American humor." The studio audiences of Johnny Carson, Phil Donahue, Mike Douglas, Merv Griffin, Dinah Shore, and many others, laughed at my funny lines and applauded my exploits, spontaneously, without being cued to do so. Sometimes they would exclaim in surprise at my narration of a particularly bold poke at the establishment, laugh, and then produce a rousing round of applause. This was my favorite such acknowledgment but I loved it all, even the one-city-per-day, eat-and-sleep-on-the-run, airport-to-hotel-to-studio-to-newspaper-to-studio-to-airport, four-weeks-at-a-clip publicity tours.

While I was becoming better known as an author, other opportunities presented themselves. I became involved in acquiring the copyrights of several independently produced made-for-television movies for a client. These contracts were extremely profitable to the producers, to the client, and to me. I was flying first class to closings offshore, living high off the hog and had developed a pretty good tan. However, the U.S. tax laws were rewritten so that many of the benefits were removed, and this source of income disappeared with the stroke of a pen. As a rigorous practitioner of the Zoroastrian precept "When thou eatest, give to the dogs, should they even bite thee," I had been improvidently squandering dollars in all directions and was having difficulty finding the handle on this particular spigot.

The money was disappearing, but I rolled with it. I was looking forward to a breakthrough in my career. My expectations for 1978 were, well, bombastic. As I told my publisher when we discussed the contract on *How to get the Upper Hand* toward the end of 1976, I had a growing sense that 1978 was to be the big year for me, the year that would bring me multimedia supersuccess, and if I could pull it off from practically a flat-on-my-back position at this stage of the game, wouldn't that taste good? And so, as Iago remarked, to work.

A woman I'd met when she was a talent coordinator with "The Mike Douglas Show" called and asked me to do some television inserts in Boston for a pilot she and her partner were producing. No money, but they'd really appreciate it. She'd acted like a pro with me when she was with "The Mike Douglas Show" so I went to Boston.

They were delightful. I loved both of them. Their pilot sold, and I pitched them the idea of an inserts series featuring guess who? Our efforts culminated in a fully executed contract with a network-owned station group, and it couldn't have come at a better time. We actually had two network-owned station groups interested, and each was aware we would sign with the first one that made us a firm offer we liked.

Segments featuring me on-camera were to be produced on locations in New York and Los Angeles. They would be telecast as part of the early evening news twice a week on the network-owned stations in each of these cities, the two top markets in the country. The other three stations owned by the network had a first refusal on the segments, and I was to do some live lead-ins and -outs in the studio in New York and Los Angeles, whether or not any of the other three stations aired the segments.

Several hundred dollars a week were to be paid by the two stations for my services and, best of all, the producers and I would own the segments. This would permit us to syndicate them, that is, to license their use on stations all over the country. We were going on the air the first week of October, 1977, and would fly out to Los Angeles as soon as we had backlogged sufficient segments in New York to cover our absence. We were feeling rather pleased with ourselves.

In addition to the obvious benefits of the contract, *Upper Hand* was scheduled for publication in January, 1978, and the segments tied directly into the book. The continuing television exposure in New York and Los Angeles couldn't help but stimulate book sales. And, with any luck, we'd be syndicating the segments in many other major markets in the country by the time the book was in the stores.

The synergy inherent in multimedia success was about to lift my career off the pad. The television exposure would make me more important as an author, and once we got a solid best seller going (not too difficult with regular and continuing national television exposure), it would build the name and lead to further developments in radio and television. Somewhere along the line, of course, a syndicated newspaper column or some national magazine columns would also fall into place. This was exactly what I told my publisher I hoped to accomplish by the time the book was published, and we'd added a small escalator in the contract if it came to pass. It wasn't all pie in the sky. Apart from all of the on-the-come goodies, there were real dollars involved in the fees for my services and in my share of the syndication of the segments, and at a minimum, the sales of the book (and the other rights in the book) had to be enhanced. The long siege of the lean years was lifting; the gamble was about to pay off.

Arthur Miller wrote the line "It certainly does take some men longer in life to get started." Well, it had taken long, but that was all right, too. It gave me a certain seasoning so that the adjustment to the Big Time would be smoother. It wasn't all bad.

My fantasies (all based on slightly optimistic projections of hard fact, or so I told myself) were going into overdrive. With the national syndication of the television segments and a strong publicity campaign driving my new book through the roof, I planned to contact a classmate of mine at law school who had become a superagent. I had been admiring his ability to put together some of the best deals in the business for his clients, at a distance, laying back until I had sufficient quid pro quo to offer him. Soon it would be time to arrange a meeting. Maybe lunch at Lutece or the Four Seasons or Christ Cella, or perhaps the steam room at his club or wherever he liked to meet to discuss big deals and a new client's career plans.

With this savvy pro in my corner to help play the hand, with my multimedia success and a book high and long on the best seller lists in both hard and soft cover, how could I miss a respectable six-figure advance on the next book; maybe even a small seven-figure amount if we made it a two-book deal (with or without a third-book option)? And, besides, by this time the money problem would be solved anyway, for by then I'd be a front-runner and on a roll, chugging into Fat City and gaining momentum with every stride of the final kick.

Right? Well, not quite. After we poured ourselves into the project wholeheartedly and several segments precisely like those we contracted to deliver were written, produced, and edited, the contract was canceled after only two segments aired in New York on the early evening news. Why the sudden cancellation after we'd spent weeks and months negotiating the contract and had delivered more than 100 percent? The segments, we were told, were "not news." I wondered aloud whether they were any more or less "news" than when the contract was signed a few days earlier. The answer we received was that it had been "a noble experiment" and I had been "really very good" but that "it just wasn't news."

This was a heavy blow and the explanation wasn't even delivered convincingly. We heard, unofficially, from a source inside the company considered reliable that one of the on-air people, as it was put, "nixed" our contract. If it happened that way, it was another one of those little daily murders that cut and maim so destructively but usually escape notice. It's only a thin scar now, but sometimes you can be so precariously perched that the smallest push, even an unexpected harsh breeze, can upset your delicate poise and send you tumbling over the brink.

The bottom line was that our contract was canceled and I was off the air. The executive with another network, who'd been interested in a similar network-station group deal and had offered to fly us to one of their stations in the Midwest to do a pilot, was no longer with the company. There would be no package of segments to syndicate, no national (or even local) television exposure to hypo sales of the book, no multimedia synergy, and our expenses in getting the project launched were not much less than the total amounts we received. It approximated a personal wipe-out for me. Thank you, Paine Webber.

Upper Hand was scheduled to be published in three months. The first printing was to be 37,500 hard-cover copies, an unusually large printing for this publishing company. There was also to be a national publicity tour, which we'd all agreed was the key to the success of the book. *Upper Hand* was highly promotable and I had already been well received on television, radio, and in the press throughout the country. I was not only contractually committed to do the tour, but it was becoming a matter of my own survival and that of my family.

On December 5, 1977, with the publication date about a

month off, I called the publicity director of the company. I sensed an ominous silence about the book and was growing a bit apprehensive. Months earlier, I'd met with the publicity director and we'd shared some ideas at a couple of lunches. I'd suggested a number of ways we might work together to greatest advantage, and the ideas had been received with apparent enthusiasm. My total availability and commitment to the tour were also set forth. Several minutes into the conversation, after a number of questions indicated nothing had been done, I learned the publicity director had resigned from the company the previous week.

Publicity directors usually don't like to be closely supervised, particularly by authors. I knew and respected that preference, but it was now apparent there simply had been no real plan and no campaign. Even the protection I thought I had from the company itself—in terms of their having announced to the trade a large first printing and a national author publicity tour, which, I reasoned, they would surely want to justify with the strongest publicity campaign they could mount for the dollars they planned to spend—was notably absent.

The pieces of a good publicity campaign mesh and interlock and build upon one another. Good reviews in the trade publications, for example, lead to wire service stories, which lead to the major national and local television and radio programs and feature stories in the press, etc. If there is no foundation, there is nothing to lock into and you produce a halfhearted effort with little effectiveness, impact, and excitement. Book sales, as well as all of the other salable rights in the book, are thereby restricted and diminished.

Coverage in the monthly magazines was no longer possible because of their long deadline requirements. Wire service stories were almost totally out of the question. In fact, a month before publication we didn't have a single trade review and not even a first draft of a publicity release had been written. I called the publisher several times, at decent intervals, but none of my calls was taken or returned. In an effort to rescue the project, now swirling ever closer to the drainage, I wrote to the publisher, layed out the facts briefly, and appealed for his help in getting the project on track.

Between the unanswered calls and my letter, I had learned the publicity campaign had been put into the hands of a part-time employee who worked out of her home on Long Island. I wrote to the publisher and suggested that it would be most helpful to hire the services of somebody who had special clout in Los Angeles, the city in which most of the important national television shows that can provide book publicity originate. In this way, we would have an opportunity to make up the lost ground. I suggested we hire a man considered by many to be the best in the business, if he were available, and offered to share the cost of his services. I also offered to call in every favor owed to me in the world and to obligate myself long into the future in order to get a strong campaign mounted. When this letter produced no response, I requested, both verbally and in writing, to meet with the publisher anywhere, at any time, to coordinate our plans, all to no avail. Without any discussion with me whatever and with the nose of the project headed toward the side of a mountain, the publisher drastically cut the print order and bailed out.

All of my assets (except for some relatively small stock holdings), several hundred thousand dollars, including the income I'd earned since leaving the network, were gone, and I was about twenty thousand dollars in debt. I was also four and a half years older than I'd been when I'd left the network, sliding down the back side of my forties, at an age when all but the latest of the late starters have long since stashed it south if they're ever going to do so. The cumulative strain, I regret to say, had affected my family and me. Weeks earlier, in a crazed outburst, a glass I'd intended to hurl against a wall tore my wife's favorite painting, one that had been a special labor of creativity and love. Shortly thereafter, she went to live with her mother. Our daughter was away at school. Feeling very much alone and as if my hand were being progressively stripped of playable strengths, I sat down and wrote this lyric and gave it to my wife the next time I saw her:

If I Say Please

Poets write of happy endings
    But they never make me glad.
Full of hurts and breaks and bendings,
    Endings only make me sad.

Without your smile my life is naught but grief;
    I die by degrees.
Is there a chance to turn another leaf
    If I say please?

The door is closed but never locked, my sweet.
    You won't need the keys.
My heart's exposed in hopes you'll hear the beat
    If I say please.

You taught me how to care.
    Even rainy days were fun.
Now, palaces are bare
    And sun is just sun.

Alone and in a mood of midnight blue,
    Beaten to my knees;
Will you come back and bring my life with you,
    If I say please?

Darling, will you come back
    and bring my life with you,
    If I say please?

The night I learned of the publisher's decision to cut in half the print order for the bookstores, I awoke from a dream. In the dream I was again living with my parents in an apartment I hadn't actually lived in for more than twenty years. I was having a conversation with a man I wasn't able to identify, at our kitchen table. I was aware of a window cleaner. I believe he was wearing a wool hat, a watch cap. Suddenly, from a point one floor above us, the man fell. There was a scream, and we heard the terrible impact as he landed about sixty feet below. When I looked down to see if he were possibly still alive, he was lying in a pool of blood. My mother, who had in reality died even before I'd moved out of this apartment, somehow seemed to be in another room of the apartment, and I suddenly awoke, terrified. I have never spent a quarter on my head, not even for a hat, and I make no claims at dream analysis, but this dream had a message I couldn't ignore. A disturbed, depressed, perhaps suicidal, mind had created this dream, and I realized I would have to try to develop a playable hand fast or hang it up.

Much of what I was and had was coming away from its moorings, and my life was flapping like a loose sail. I was also heartsick. My life had become a series of unfulfilling collisions, a long series of conflicts and controversies. I was separating myself from others, taking myself almost off the curve of humanity itself. As "the world's most successful complainer," I had felt the challenge of being the town's fastest gun, but I was getting older, gaining a better perspective on myself, and I'd lost the taste for fast drawing.

Perhaps desperately, I wanted to find my way back to myself and my original hopes and dreams. It was as if I could barely hear the most exquisite music. Almost inaudible, if I strained I could pick it up only faintly, indistinctly, and it moved me to tears of joy. I knew this sound was the music I wanted and had to have in my life, but I couldn't receive it any better on any of my tuner dials no matter how hard I tried, and I was too sad and unenlightened to realize I was the source of the music for which I yearned.

With the clock ticking as loudly as I've ever heard it, I decided to stop fighting the maze, to stop fighting the world, to stop fighting myself, to simply stop everything and let go. After a while I began to relate more closely and in a different way with everything that came before me, and my understanding and appreciation of other people, animals, plants, even of inanimate objects, seemed deeper and more authentic. Slowly, the patterns of my life began to change. I was relearning myself and understanding how that self related to and in the world. The ice began to break, and spring, a little late that year, finally arrived.

As the personal relationships in my life grew closer and deeper and more real, the business side also began to function better. For example, in a one-week period in mid-April, 1978, *Upper Hand* ground almost to a halt with a net of twenty copies shipped and billed. However, with a great deal of help from friends, for which I am profoundly grateful, its life supports held, and during the last week of May, 1978, more than nine thousand net copies were shipped and billed and my gross income that week from all sources exceeded forty thousand dollars.

The dream of multimedia success has not been abandoned. I have a new publisher. There is a sense of team effort. The lines of communication are open, and my contribution is welcome. Segments featuring me (like those that were "not news") are being telecast regularly on a local television station. Again, there is a sense of family, of belonging. I am also writing a regular column for a national magazine and am on its editorial board. Here, too, the editor and publisher have been a great pleasure to know. One of my books is being developed by a major supplier as a prime-time network television comedy series, and one of my closest and dearest friends is the creative head of the project. This is a whole new way of thinking and expression for "the world's most successful complainer," and I love it. My family, I'm delighted to report, are also well and happy. The past is over and the present is better and better. My wife is back and smiling again and the relationship, like a cleanly broken bone that heals and bonds properly, is stronger than ever. Our daughter, off to a jumping competition in Ireland as this is being written, will return to her senior year at college.

I am not a clergyperson or a doctor, and some may

consider it presumptuous of me to write a book such as this. I can understand that point of view, and, in fact, this was one of the first questions I asked myself when I began to think about this project. We are living in an age in which many have come to question and to tune out the voices of the accredited, the sanctified, the authoritative and to turn instead to people they know or trust, or simply to other people like themselves who have covered the same terrain at ground level. I think this is a positive development.

I'd also read my share of books by clergypeople and doctors, and they'd done little, if anything, to change my life for the better. In fact, if I may say so without giving offense, some of the better popular song lyrics have done more for me. The formal education I'd received in excellent schools and universities was equally inadequate in providing me with the knowledge and the attitude I would need to lead a happy, productive life. So, too, the sum of my experience had provided virtually nothing with which to make my life work particularly well, especially if I happened to get out of the gate with less than a great start. In sum, I had a wonderful mind and body but there was no owner's manual in sight.

What I'm attempting in these pages is to offer some person-to-person notes and observations and thoughts along the lines I wish to God somebody had offered to me earlier in the game. As readers of my other books know, I have always written from the bedrock of my own concrete experience. The *Complaints* book came directly from my life as "the world's most successful complainer." My book on the subject of listed stock options was based on a method of trading I created in taking fifty-one consecutive profits with my own money in the listed stock options markets within a period of five months. *Upper Hand* was a distillation of methods and techniques, fully kitchen-tested by its author, that anybody could use to muzzle a lot of the nonsense in our lives.

In putting together the shards and shreds of my battered position and weaving them into a vital, creative, productive, rewarding life, I discovered a number of significant signposts that had previously been completely obscured or so insufficiently illuminated as to ensure they would be missed at the normal traveling speed through life. I've collected and organized them and pass them along here in the hope and belief that if these signposts were able to guide me out of deepening quicksand, they may also guide others on firmer, or, if such is the case, equally treacherous ground.

How to Make Things Go Your Way is a synthesis of everything I've seen work for the most successful people I know (and which I've been successfully putting to work) as well as all of the pitfalls and sand traps to be avoided that keep most of us way back in the pack (and kept me an also-ran for years). The presentation is nontechnical, and it is recommended for people of all ages. This, then, is a loving attempt at presenting the owner's manual I wish had been given to me as soon as I was old enough to read.

**Oh, Ben, how did you do it?
What is the answer?**

Arthur Miller
Death of a Salesman

Personal Relationships

When Willy Loman repeatedly asked his more successful brother, Ben, what the secret of success was, we were touched. Poor Willy was only grasping at straws. How could there really be such a secret? We knew there was no such thing. Well, I think there actually is such a secret. The starting point for this opinion was a statement made by a man I knew who was president of one of the most successful of the Fortune 500 companies. The statement sounded almost ludicrous when I first heard it. However, it seemed to mean so much to him I decided to hold it up to the light a few times and turn it about so I could view it from other points of view.

"People," he said, "do business with people with whom they like to do business." That's the nub of it. There are people with whom we *enjoy* doing business. We like to have them about us. They make us feel good. Think about it for a moment. Are the most successful people you know the ones with the highest intelligence quotients? Are they the best educated? Are they really the most competent people available to do their particular jobs? Make your own informal survey.

Aren't there lots of more intelligent, better educated, more able people who aren't doing half as well?

To oversimplify, imagine there are two entrances to a building you visit every day. One entrance is guarded by somebody who somehow causes a pain in your head every time you enter and leave through the door he guards. Every time you pass the other guard, however, a feeling of well-being, of salubriousness, rises within you and you smile. In fact, even before you reach this guard, you begin to breathe more freely and take bigger steps in anticipation of how good you're about to feel. Which door are you going to use, even if it's a little out of your way?

Not only do people do business with those with whom they like to do business, they also hire and promote them. Have you, for example, ever been better qualified for a job or promotion somebody else received? People also marry and stay married to (or live with and continue to live with) people they like to have about them. The same principle applies to the entire range of personal relationships. We know the meek shall inherit the earth, but I can tell you these people get it *inter vivos*. They sail right through mud.

They are also in great demand socially, obliged by schedule conflicts to turn down more invitations then they can accept. Favors and courtesies are continually showered upon them. Their pets thrive; their plants flourish, and cuttings of them live forever. Their soufflés invariably rise; their deals close. Taxis stop at their feet even before they're hailed. Their smiles calm even the half-crazed, and both Scrooge and Silas Marner contribute bountifully to their charities at first request, albeit anonymously, of course. Their telephones are continually ringing with good news and opportunities, and there is almost complete unanimity among people who hold a broad spectrum of opinion on other subjects that these are the people most liked, the people in whose company they feel good about themselves. There is, alas, the same consensus that certain other people put us off, make us feel uncomfortable and we prefer to avoid them.

Why this is so, how it works, and what we can do to become one of the favored group is worth investigating. First, however, if you have already rejected this thesis because you have thought of one or two exceptions to the rule, please take a moment and reconsider. Think of the last occasion on which a business or social relationship proved to be extremely unsatisfactory, disappointing, and/or intensely painful. Would it be fair to say that the same sort of thinking, namely, the attempt to make oneself right and one or more others wrong, was precisely the root cause of whatever precipitated the extremely bad bottom line result?

Granted, you may be able to think of a couple of exceptions. Consider, however, that if you want to hit one out of the park, you've got to give the pitcher permission to go through his or her motions. If you keep taking yourself out of the batter's box because you don't like the pitcher's motion, you're not going to get any swings at the ball. Some people keep themselves thus sidelined when they could be putting out all-star performances. There are even some who not only take themselves out of the lineup, they stop the game for everybody else, too. In this latter group may be included lawyers who can prevent the consummation of any deal, those for whom suitors of people close to them are never good enough, cynics who profess to be uninterested in anything, and hordes of self-destructive others who will assure the failure of everything with which they become involved.

Based on a great deal of close observation, I am convinced that the attitude and character of the participants, not their abilities, determine the outcome of most encounters. There is an instructive scene between Paul Newman and George C. Scott in the film *The Hustler* that well illustrates this point. Newman, as Fast Eddie, can't understand why he lost the match to Minnesota Fats, played by Jackie Gleason. I don't have the exact lines before me, but to paraphrase Newman: "I know I have more talent. How come I lost?" Whereupon Scott replies something like: "Kid, everybody has talent. He had character."

What is it about the people whose personal relationships are successful that makes others want to have them about? Why do we feel good about ourselves in their presence and willingly enter into business and social relationships with them? Why do these relationships have the greatest chances for success? Why, conversely, do we shrink from becoming involved with some people? What are we reacting to about them that puts us off? Do successful people communicate to us specific character traits and attitudes not found among the self-defeating and the unsuccessful, and vice versa? Based on what I've observed from my particular perch in the crow's nest, there are definite clusters of similarities among the successful and significantly different clusters of similarities found among the less than successful. We can expect to find valuable clues as to why some people create for themselves a life that works beautifully while others consistently jam their own mechanisms, in their interpersonal behavior.

We've already seen, in passing, one characteristic that separates the successful people from the unsuccessful. The latter have the insatiable need to make themselves right and to make others wrong. This unenlightened attitude is a heavy-duty poison that kills relationships on contact. Those afflicted with this disease of the spirit tend to take things extremely literally, become self-righteous and recriminatory if the commas and footnotes of a relationship or a deal are not strictly adhered to, make inordinate, perfectionistic demands on themselves and others, and can cut through goodness and beauty like a laser to find some insignificant flaw even in a masterwork. It is not enough that they are right and you are wrong. You must acknowledge it in writing, under oath, and get it notarized for them, even on Sundays and holidays. With this approach, they have little difficulty tipping over canoes anchored in glacial ice. Relationships less solidly fixed are simply blown out of the water.

Successful people, on the other hand, know how to score points without having to take them away from anybody else. Whether you are on their team or on the other side of the table, they can find a way for everybody to win. This is the most efficient way to play the game and perhaps the only route to long-term success, for people who are made wrong or trampled have a vested interest in finding ingenious ways to upset agreements thought already put to bed.

Disruptive behavior is another way to get others to head for the exits. Rooms people who exhibit such behavior enter are never at the proper temperature, and the air currents, objectionably stale or drafty, must be altered at once. Their personal preferences are of supreme importance. If somebody half a football field away is smoking, they will soon be coughing and grimacing. Your Karistan upsets their allergy and will surely bring on an attack unless it is immediately rolled up and removed from their lines of sight. This latter sense is delicate, too, and even indirect lighting creates an unbearable glare. They are also sensitive to decibels. Your pet invariably gives them a problem and must be placed under immediate house arrest. This is not all to the bad, however, for pets tend to bristle in their presence and wish to escape, sometimes going to the extreme of flinging themselves from closed windows, shards of glass embedded in their flanks.

On a good day, a practiced disruptive in full stride can stop a factory of Swiss watches with a single frown. They are also affronted and made uncomfortable if the focus of conversation strays from them, if only temporarily. Even an all-expenses-paid vacation to Shangri-La will be found wanting by them. Inside of a fortnight in their presence, a cadre of monks and lamas, bordering on exhaustion and hysteria induced by their incessant demands, would be hopelessly hooked on tranquilizers, lovingly transported over the mountains by marathon runners.

Another featured player in our cast of nonsuccesses is the naysayer. This type is easily identified for they won't sally forth into society without a pair of jeweler's loupes firmly embedded in their eye sockets. Highly skilled at analyzing fine print, gifted Cassandras can wither everything that comes under their jaundiced gaze. They are often the product of an unresolved disappointment, breach of faith, rejection, or loss of love early in life, and everybody they subsequently meet is placed under suspicion and held at bay. Trust and closeness are intolerable. They can't afford to take chances for fear of a possible repetition of the original pain. Social relationships with those so afflicted are doomed. The business side of their lives is also stunted. Either dismissed out of hand or minutely dissected and found wanting, no business opportunity is judged genuine or worthwhile. In time, these people are reduced to associating with an ever-decreasing number of like-minded others who continue to buttress each other's unfulfilled lives with mutually corroborating tales of pain, loss, injustice, and betrayal.

Similarly, those who repeatedly fail to keep their agreements and commitments (procrastinators, the chronically late, the forgetful, the renegotiators, the untruthful, etc.) drastically limit their lives and adversely affect others. Those who deal by shows of strength, threats, tantrums, bullying, and other communications studded with exclamation points need not detain us here. Their immoderate approach is as inappropriate as it is self-defeating. Those who are coerced by them are usually too weak to add any value to the relationship, while those who might have been of help are likely to decline the opportunity and stay well out of earshot.

In this short, by no means exhaustive, list are many of the unattractive ways we, and/or others, behave. Such conduct provides an irritating diet of weeds and wild grasses—sour bulk and no nourishment. Human relationships fed on such staples cannot grow and develop and blossom. If good business, social, romantic, and familial relationships are the keys to our own happiness and success, we must learn to replace self-defeating behavior with attitudes and actions that will work for us. Many of us have acquired our self-defeating methods from well-intentioned parents who, more likely than not, did not realize they were providing their offspring with unworkable and disserving models. Some of us, alas, are handing down these family heirlooms to our own progeny.

If we study the ways successful people, those whose lives

are working optimally, conduct themselves with others, we can learn to use some of their methods and fashion some new and more invigorating rhythms for ourselves. Surely it makes more sense to look at what works instead of simply repeating versions and variations of what doesn't work. Joseph Wood Krutch put it well: "We have been deluded by the fact that the methods employed for the study of man have been, for the most part, those originally devised for the study of machines or the study of rats, and are capable, therefore, of detecting and measuring only those characteristics which the three do have in common."

One marvelous quality found among the people whose lives work is that they relate to, and appreciate, us as we are. They experience people not as utensils, which may be useful for this or that purpose, but as they are in their own nature. They take us as they find us, and they permit us to grow at our own rate. They don't continually judge us and find us wanting. They seek out points and areas of agreement and are able to build on these to reduce the separations between us and themselves and bring us closer. They are aware that the similarities among people bulk so much larger than the differences. They do not criticize. They do not volunteer advice. They are not constantly striving to manipulate or control us. What is, is good enough to work with and it will get better through their efforts. They have nothing to fear and are free to present themselves as they are. They are confident they can affect the outcome of a situation or event, and with this attitude and their own contribution to the particular project at hand, they repeatedly do so, moving from one successful result to another.

Successful people also put themselves into relationships whole-heartedly. To do otherwise, that is, to hold themselves apart from relationships, to try to preserve themselves from change, from risk, from life itself, would chill and destroy the relationships. They also seem to have a genuine liking for themselves and others, and their feelings for others take nothing away from their feelings for themselves. There is no subservience in their relationships. Theirs are relationships of equality, relationships that offer the best chances for growth despite the individual differences of the parties and their differing individual rates of growth. To paraphrase a line from Shakespeare's *Julius Caesar*: "It's not that they love themselves less; they love others more."

Successful people (used here interchangeably with "people who have successful relationships") are able to see the overview, the big picture, the doughnut. Others, less successful, concern themselves with their own locked-in points of view, the tiniest details, the hole. The former have an energy, an aliveness, that drives the machinery forward, that keeps everything and everybody in motion, that attracts others and produces much greater results in concert than the various sums of that which could be achieved separately. This creative force is expressed as enthusiasm and it is noticeably absent from the lives of those whose dreams have faded and grown dim.

Another cluster of characteristics successful people share is an openness, an openmindedness, an approachability, a willingness to believe in the possible, a seemingly incongruous naïveté, an unselfconsciousness and a sense of humor. They are aware that circumstances change but that circumstances, however good or bad, are only circumstances. How they will deal with the circumstances, not the circumstances themselves, is what is important and they are confident they will be able to handle whatever changes occur. The strength of their personal relationships derives not from toughness but from flexibility.

They do not foreclose possibilities. They are willing to reexamine decisions already made in order to get a better result. When, for example, Elia Kazan was directing the film *On the Waterfront*, he and producer Sam Spiegel used to hold regular meetings. Occasionally, Mr. Spiegel would rethink a particular decision they had reached and he would go back to Mr. Kazan and say: "Let's look at it again." The discussion was reopened, and they both agree the result was a better film.

There is an absence of fixing blame, of making other people wrong, of bad-mouthing others, among successful people. Despite their successes, they are not always center-stage, discussing at length their problems, plans, and accomplishments. They are skillful, active listeners, willing to acknowledge others, ready to demonstrate their understanding of the point of view being expressed and able to ask for additional information gently and without producing conflict. Above all, those who are successful (who have successful personal relationships) have a frame of mind, a mental set, that makes it all right for them to be successful (to have successful personal relationships). They expect success, they accept it, they are at ease with it.

The converse is also true. Those who are unsuccessful (who have unsuccessful personal relationships) have a frame of mind, a mental set, that makes it not all right for them to be successful (to have successful personal relationships). Some of these people also consider it not all right for others to be successful and to have successful personal relationships. Unsuccessful people carry with them feelings of unworthiness which are often unknown, unacknowledged, elusive, deeply buried. Their unsuccessful pasts determine their futures.

In attempting to take control of my own life, I considered this latter possibility several times and rejected its application to me each time save the last. On paper my stats weren't too bad. I was extremely intelligent and had been checked out in private and group tests with IQs that ranged from 154 to 195. I had three degrees from excellent schools. I was attractive, articulate, had a sense of humor, and possessed most of the Boy Scout virtues with the notable exception of thrift. I even had a pretty good philosophical grounding, or so I thought, and this added to my disappointment with myself that I had reached the point at which I was considering throwing in the hand. Why hadn't it turned out as I'd hoped and dreamed? Was my past determing my future? If so, was there a way for me (and others) to free ourselves from the grip of the past and create a more successful pattern for our lives?

If I were defeating myself for reasons not yet clear, maybe

I could reach back, find the hidden short circuits, and put them right. As the flight recorder of a downed aircraft is much sought after, not only for the insights it may provide as to the cause of any mechanical malfunction, but also for the valuable information it may contain which might eliminate future mishaps, so, too, might I (and others) be helped by a careful review of our own "flight recorder." Thus, if I could locate it among the scattered wreckage, I might not only be able to find the old, festering wounds and give them a chance to heal, but I might also learn how to correct much pilot error I still carried within my own internal guidance systems. It was worth a try and there certainly didn't seem to be very much to lose. As with flight recorders, the clues, not the prose, are of significance. The references are rather personal and are passed along not by way of demonstrating the author's self-indulgence, but in order to document and better explain a method I found extremely helpful and which may be of benefit to others.

On a clear, subfreezing winter morning, I walked the mile and a half to Grand Central Station and bought a round-trip ticket for about five dollars that put me on the next train out of the depot. I wanted to have a quiet conversation with myself and decided it would be easier to do so if I went to a location away from telephones and one that had no past associations for me. Any town with which I was unfamiliar would do.

I used to rummage through second-hand bookstores and buy old and dusty physics textbooks, and I enjoyed experimenting with laboratory equipment and chemicals when I was a kid, but that was a long time ago. This was to be a completely different kind of experiment. Was it foolish to take a two-and-a-half-dollar train ride to a place I'd never set foot on, in search of myself, and a return ticket to the human continuum? What were the chances? I knew people who'd spent many years in analysis with no dramatic results to report. How could I reasonably expect some kind of instant conversion for myself, and conversion to what? And yet . . . the country was in a "born again" fervor, wasn't it? Weren't people experiencing life-changing results? A new spiritual awareness was abroad in the land, and if I opened myself to it, maybe . . . or was this only wishful thinking?

I brought along a composition notebook, the kind I'd used in grammar school, with bound, blue-lined pages, a red-lined margin, and black and white, mottled covers. The purpose of the bound pages was to keep all the notes I intended to take intact so that if they failed to produce their magic at once, I'd have a chance to go over the material again. The notebook also had an association with my childhood. I thought it would help me remember those early years and lead me more easily to what was separating me from other people. The connection between my traveling on a railroad track and my wanting to put my life on track crossed my mind, but I would leave the symbols for much later. For the moment, I wanted to get in touch with the past and learn how my attitudes toward myself and other people had developed. This, I was reasonably sure, was at the core of my difficulties, where help was most needed and where it would do the most good.

As the train left the terminal, I began to feel better. I'd done a fair amount of writing on trains and airplanes and knew of professional writers who used such trips as sure cures for writer's block when all else failed them. Long walks had the same effect on some people. Perhaps the motion has a way of stimulating thought.

I liked the idea of looking for the flight recorder of a downed plane. Following that analogy a bit father, I decided to pursue two separate lines of inquiry: "mechanical failure" and "pilot error." I opened the notebook so that I had two blank pages before me. In this way I could see more easily how the two pages compared if I later wanted to look at both as a whole. On the left page, under "mechanical failure," I would seek to uncover and list the early cuts and bruises my psyche had received. I would consider each of them separately in order to determine whether these wounds had properly healed or were festering and still hurting me. The silent, submerged, still damaged (and damaging) areas would register as "hot spots" and reveal themselves by producing a strong emotional response. This response would be cathartic. Each old wound would be drained and cleansed, and a healing process would begin, or so I hoped.

On the facing page of the notebook I would list, under "pilot error," those attitudes, character traits, and bits of behavior I had acquired that were characteristic of either of my parents and that I would now judge to be detrimental to good personal relationships. I would try to find connections between the items listed and any bad results I'd experienced in dealing with other people. Problem areas would become apparent in the same way; i.e., by their ability to produce a strong emotional response in me. I would underline the "hot spots" on both pages and monitor their effects on future relationships.

As I alighted from the train, the sun was shining but it was a bitter cold wintry day. I headed for the relative tranquility of the more prosperous side of the railroad tracks, found a park bench, turned up my coat collar, took off my gloves, and began to get into the experiment. I allowed my thoughts to drift back to my childhood. . . .

Most of the items on my two lists were light-years away, long burned out and cold, no longer troubling me. The heat came from my early relationship with my father. My earliest memories of my father were of him sitting in "his" chair reading *The New York Times*, the paper obscuring his face from view, further isolating me from his company. When I was about four, I noticed my father shaving with a safety razor, with the bathroom door open. I asked why he put that white stuff on his face only to take it off shortly thereafter; why put it on in the first place? My father apparently took this as either a foolish question or an attempt by a four-year-old to put him on, for his face contorted in an unfriendly grimace and he slammed the door in my face. I happen to throw a baseball left-handed, a fact that appeared not to register with my father, as he bought me a baseball glove for the wrong hand when I was about nine, and, significantly, I didn't tell him about it until I was twenty-three.

My mother hadn't produced any "mechanical failures" of

note. In reviewing the list of "pilot errors"—those attitudes, character traits, and bits of behavior which hadn't worked for my parents—I discovered I'd acquired several that were keeping me apart from others and thus working against my interests.

The next step of the experiment called for me to understand the items on both lists that produced "hot spots" from the point of view of the person who'd caused and/or committed them. This was to take the form of several separate "conversations" between myself and the other person, in which I would attempt to explain the other person's point of view as well as my own. I would, in effect, ask the other person why he'd acted as he had, and listen carefully and respectfully to the explanation I would provide. This exercise produced a number of highly charged emotional moments and several new insights about my father and myself.

I learned that my father did not want a second child, especially at that time, the beginning of the Great Depression. His own father had considered himself something of a playboy, and he'd left the family from time to time. My father, the eldest of five children had taken up the slack by helping to supply income.

My father saw himself as always at sea, fighting the tides, trying to stay afloat, essentially alone in an alien environment, struggling to forge ahead, taking gambles with his slender resources and usually seeing them not pay off, setting himself apart from others by a thinly disguised wall of fear and feelings of inadequacy and by his characteristic undemonstrativeness of affection. I saw, for the first time, the connection between my father's attitude toward me and the fact that I never had any biological children of my own (I had adopted my wife's child by a prior marriage). Had I reached this insight and loosed its grip on me earlier, I am sure my point of view in the conversations I'd had with my wife about having another child would have been entirely different.

The next step in the experiment required an understanding and an acceptance that what had been done, particularly by my father, had been unnecessary and hurtful but that he had been operating under many handicaps and limitations. I believed this. He didn't have to handle many of the situations the way he had. By so doing, he had damaged both his children and his wife. However, notwithstanding the distance he maintained between himself and those who should have been closest to him, he had not intended the harmful results. I could understand and forgive him at last. There was no way I could actually have this conversation with either of my parents for they were both deceased.

I had picked up many of my father's faults but not all, and those I had contracted were of a milder form. And my daughter was symptom-free of the list, so they had not been transmitted any farther. As I could understand and forgive my father's shortcomings, so, too, could I understand and forgive myself. There were many other insights received that day that illuminated where I was and how I got there and I felt immeasurably better for the experience.

On the ride home, I reread the lists and spent some time thinking about the items I'd checked, the ones that had produced the emotional "hot spots." They were cooler now. The healing process, begun at last by lancing these old wounds, would continue.

The memories would remain, but their ability to affect my actions would grow progressively weaker. The next time I felt called upon to react in some familiar but self-destructive way, I would be there to counsel myself in loving, patient, and understanding language. The other person might well be in the wrong and I in the right, but as an exercise I would not overreact. The next time it would be even easier to handle the same kind of situation.

If I wanted to go off by myself in the midst of other people, say at a party, I would counsel myself to stay and get into the social flow of the action in the same patient, loving, and understanding way. It would be easier the next time. In the same way, I would monitor the effects on my relationships of every underlined item on both lists. By thus "leaning against the wind" in these situations that had previously controlled my actions in self-destructive ways, I would move toward the norm, toward fulfilling, rewarding, successful personal relationships. I understood and liked myself in a new way and was rooting for myself as never before.

When I reached Grand Central Station, I was feeling much lighter. My senses seemed keener, more attuned, and I was much more aware of others. I felt a great compassion for, and a new kind of understanding of, the people I saw in the terminal and on my way home, and, although the temperature was still hovering at about ninteen degrees, I felt warm.

> A man that's got something to say
> don't need all week to make his point.
>
> Joe Louis

Communication

The primitive grunts, gestures, and cave paintings that were the principal means our ancestors had for exchanging information have been augmented over the years by a dazzling array of modes and means, tools and technologies for communicating in scores of languages. We can communicate not only with one another, but with other species, other planets, with machines, and even our machines have learned to talk to us and with other machines.

We have satellites, cables, microwave relays, wires, optical fibers. We communicate face to face, over telephone and telegraph lines, by microphone and megaphone, by mail and by hand. We advertise, we sell, we present, we promote, we publicize, we subscribe, we mail-order. We use facsimiles, telegrams, holograms, heliograms, linotype, teletype, hype. We typewrite, we skywrite, we photocopy, we use video and audio tapes and discs, we film and microfiche, we store data, we examine computer printouts, we go to drive-ins and feed jukeboxes, we punch cards. Neologisms to describe new communications methods and techniques are continually coined.

We use lasers and masers and stargazers, cassettes and carrier pigeons, wrappers and packaging. We sleep-learn. We communicate by status symbols, we adorn our bodies with jewelry, clothing, facial hair, suntan, paint, powder, masks, and tattoos. We are into ESP. We communicate by road signs and billboards, contests and competitions, drumbeats and puffs of smoke.

We use signals and semaphores, lead sheets, player pianos and spray cans, signs, seals and symbols, and soap boxes of all sizes. We orate, we write graffiti, we dance, we sing, we listen to music, we paint, we sculpt, we go to the theater. We read textbooks and matchbooks, communicate subliminally, by smell, by touch, even by silence. We have public and private hearings, assemblies, forums. Our communications are verbal and nonverbal, subtle, hidden, obvious, blatant. We laugh, we cry, we mime, we rhyme. We use polygraphs, phonographs, illusions, labels, logos, and movies, both sound and silent. We go to court, we listen to pitchpeople. We refer to maps and manuals and carry ID. We find meaning in ancient architectural formations and decipher the languages of other species. We communicate up close and at a distance, one to many, many to one, one to one, many to many. We mediate, arbitrate, educate, and legislate. We communicate by acts, deeds and by example.

We use codes, secret and conventional. Finger paints and voiceprints tell us something. We have couriers and calling cards, letters, handbills and circulars, periodicals, stickers, toys, buttons, beads, pennants, banners, flags, placards, car cards, and sound trucks, and we post bills. We yodel and whistle, we sermonize, we even use formations of people. We cheer, we applaud, we hoot and holler, we moan and boo. We discover dead languages and Dead Sea scrolls.

We use jingles and promos, rubber stamps and postage stamps, name tags, and dogtags, sandwich boards and sign language, body language, stenography, transcriptions, inscriptions, dictographs and dictaphones, engravings, embossings, imprints, winks and tickles, hugs and kisses, handshakes and high signs, poetry and press releases, theme music and segue cues, X rays and death rays. We communicate by statute, rule, ordinance, regulation, proclamation, ultimatum, fiat, and fait accompli. We confront with weaponry, we eyeball, we stonewall, we let it all hang out. We assault, we insult, we create "images," we set in stone or in sand, we use subtitles, calls and decals, stencils and pencils, mantras, mandates and mandalas, a.m. and f.m., totems and taboos, myths and shibboleths, legends, chants, hymns, prayers and anthems.

We use slogans and trademarks, we read prospectuses and reports. We send candygrams, write anagrams and hexagrams, cryptograms and thermograms, listen to spirit-rapping and study ouija boards, wear iron-ons and put on light shows. We are licensed and certified and we use ink, invisible and magnetic. We use slides and filmstrips, watch television and home movies. We even send messages in bottles and we are into multimedia.

The list is long and growing. The resultant din is so pervasive there is a rising premium on "getting away from it all." We take our telephones off their respective hooks or have our calls screened. Some pay a monthly fee for unlisted numbers and post office boxes. We are "not in" to unannounced or uninvited visitors. We hang "do not disturb" signs; we meditate. We guard our sleep with "white" noises. Unanswered mail, memos, and calls gradually slide into oblivion. Our attention spans continue to shrink. We sometimes forget whom we called while their telephone is ringing. We demand summaries and digests. All we need have is "the flavor." We insist on "the bottom line" at the top. We are impatient. We get bored. Our souls ache.

Most of our social and business communications are vaguely disappointing, and even our more personal conversations are hollow. As in junk food, there is little nourishment to sustain us in the junk communication, composed, for the most part, of empty words and phrases, signifying little, and sugared over and puffed to indecorous length. Increasingly, our senses and sensibilities are numbed by a communications overload which manages to touch us only superficially and peripherally most of the time. We detect in many of them an attempt to manipulate or control us. We are aware of the insincerity, the lack of care for us. We know of the existence of cue cards, "applause" signs, and "laugh tracks." We sense the attempt to treat us as utensils, to use us for some preconceived purpose, to entice us to buy, to urge us to work harder, to get our vote or contribution, to make us respond in myriad ways that benefit an interest other than our own.

We are dissatisfied with mass communications, and we also seem to have lost the ability to speak to one another. Our conversations are usually lifeless and perfunctory. We are rarely moved by a direct exchange with another human being. Why do we have so much difficulty in expressing our thoughts and feelings in ways that facilitate our working and playing together in harmony and abundance? Why do we isolate ourselves from one another in virtually airtight membranes? Why do other people "turn us off" or produce "bad vibes"? Even children are strangers, separated from their parents by a "generation gap."

If a single unifying principle were applied to the basic unit of our everyday, immediate, two-way, personal, verbal exchanges—our conversations—we could produce a climate for miraculous changes in our lives. In such conversations lie innumerable opportunities for cooperative ventures of almost limitless variety, and your share of the benefits of such joining of efforts is likely to be several times greater than the net results of trying to go it alone or to fight the world.

There was a recent feature story in a Canadian newspaper about two gentlemen, aged sixty-two and seventy-three, who own and manage a shipbuilding business in Newfoundland. It came into being as a direct result of a conversation during a chance meeting at the local post office seven years earlier. In the words of the company president:

"Me and Leas were talking about one thing and another and we eventually got around to the shipyard. Both of us felt it was a crying shame that the yard had been idle for over two years and we decided to do something about it—then and there."

That single conversation was the starting point for what is now a multimillion-dollar business with forty-seven employees. It is interesting to note that in its thirty-five-year prior history, three other owners had tried to operate that shipyard and failed.

Your ability to talk to other people is fundamental to increasing your own happiness and success. As you improve your ability to exchange your thoughts and feelings with others, you improve the quality of your life. Most people yearn for the opportunity to present themselves in conversation as they are, and to be understood and accepted as they are. Most of us welcome an authentic exchange without the encumbering censorship we impose on ourselves. Sparkling drawing-room dialogue is not the point. What most of want is to be sending and to be received on precisely the same wavelength.

Some people are able to relate to others in this way without difficulty, and do so regularly. Others set up barriers that block meaningful conversation. In time, the barriers become almost automatic, imposing a kind of mental and spiritual quarantine on the person behind them. There are, fortunately, easily learned ways to become conscious of these walls and to break through them to human contact. Let's look at one simple principle and some methods and techniques, all readily put into practice and mastered in everyday encounters, for dramatically improving the quality of conversational exchanges.

The principle is simply stated: Whatever removes the separations between you and others is a plus; whatever heightens or increases these separations is a minus. Without regard to the content, what are the conditions in conversational settings that bring people closer together or that produce separations? The ideal conversational setting is "a safe space."

and/or thanks. It is a verbal pat on the back you give another person. If somebody cooked, or supervised the cooking of, a meal or a dish you enjoy, you acknowledge it. If somebody did you a favor, or tried to, you express your appreciation. Acknowledgment used to be one of my failings. As "the world's most successful complainer," I had the uncanny ability to hone in from any angle on what was wrong, however microscopic (and in my sole judgment, of course), and to ignore what was right.

It is important to look for opportunities to acknowledge others and to do so whenever possible, without dissembling. Acknowledgments should not be elaborate or flowery, and they should not be addressed to anybody other than the person (or persons) you are acknowledging. It is meant to be a simple, genuine, and natural statement. To cite a mundane example, if your mate happens to cook an elaborate dinner or tries a new recipe, you might acknowledge it by saying, "Marge (or Harry), that was delicious. I don't know how you find the time to be such a great chef."

As indicated above, I used to be one of the people who were more likely to comment on what they didn't appreciate than what they did. This is clearly against our principle. There are ways to disagree or take exception without becoming divisive that we can look at later, but agreement is a much more important element. It is obviously another stabilizing factor in relationships; it tends to remove separations between yourself and others and makes for greater intimacy.

If you can do so without equivocation or loss of integrity, provide verbal reassurance by expressing agreement wherever possible. It is also a good way to "take the floor": "I agree with that, George" (and here you lay in briefly and in your own words the essence of what you agree with in George's position). It is now easy to add to George's statement: "And I think we should add this." You and George (and perhaps the others as well) are now "we," a team instead of factions disputing with one another. It is clear that reinforcing an expressed view, as in this example, will be received as a friendly gesture, whereas a direct challenge or the putting in question of another person's self-image or position will be interpreted as a hostile act.

Should you disagree and find it necessary to say so (which shouldn't be every time you find something with which to disagree), as you become more skillful at conversation, you may do so without head-on confrontations. I used to be a vocal disagreer and considered it a loss of integrity if I found something to disagree about and didn't disclose it. I didn't understand the concept of a conversation in the same way I do now. In my present view, a conversation is an opportunity to get to know another person (or persons) and an opportunity for others to get to know me. Conversations are vehicles for exchanging thoughts and feelings and ideas, for reducing separations, and for discovering new opportunities to share present and future possibilities that may come into being spontaneously. For me to interrupt the flow to voice certain disagreements is a disservice to the conversation and the parties to it. Spontaneity and creativity deserve a better environment. If it becomes necessary to take exception to something, there will be ample opportunity to do so. I am not going to act out of harmony with my own character and I am not going to delude or deceive anybody about what I think. But, just as I am willing to "suspend disbelief" when I enter a theater, I am willing to give the speaker the benefit of the doubt and much latitude, for the sake of the conversation, before any objections from me. Sometimes, by so doing, the other person may clarify what was said so that no objection need be interposed. If not, my right to interrupt to seek clarification and/or to disagree is not waived, as it might be in a courtroom; it remains intact.

In disagreeing, it is a good idea to first demonstrate your understanding of what the other person has said and to express agreement with any portions with which you happen to agree, before noting your objection. If possible, look for some common ground that would compose or resolve the difference.

If none presents itself, you may at least suggest the possibility. For example, let's suppose you are a man and are having lunch with a male friend downtown, whose wife and he were your hosts at a party three weeks earlier. You and your wife like the other couple very much, and you enjoyed the party. In the spirit of good fellowship, but without discussing it with your wife, you invite him and his wife to your house for dinner the following Saturday evening. You are now discussing it with your wife, and she points out that she had made some other plans for that Saturday afternoon and would have preferred to invite the other couple at a more convenient time. You, however, feel committed and want to keep the dinner date, but you realize you ought to have discussed it with your wife before extending the invitation.

First, you will want to demonstrate to your wife that you understand her point of view and agree with it:

"I'm very sorry, Marge. You're right. It was impulsive of me to invite the Bakers for dinner without first discussing it with you, and I can understand how jammed up your day would be."

You are playing back her point of view in your own words and showing you understand her and admit she's right. This will have a defusing effect. You are not confronting, insisting, demanding, and raising the level or the temperature of the disagreement. Now, if you're satisfied from her verbal or nonverbal response that you have actually contained the original objection, you are ready to state your point of view and to try to resolve the difference:

"But it's going to be very embarrassing for me to call Frank and cancel. And I know how much you like Betty and Frank. Maybe we could invite them to the theater and a restaurant downtown and come back here for dessert afterwards. What do you think?"

First, you have tried to dissipate some of the heat by paying attention while your wife was speaking and by expressing your understanding of her point of view and agreeing with her. You then expressed your own feelings; you told her how embarrassing it would be for you to cancel the invitation. You've reminded her of her positive feelings for the other couple. You've suggested a possible way to resolve the disagreement and, finally, you've asked for her thoughts. You made an honest mistake that produced an inconvenience for your wife, but you're not in a war of words over it. You're approaching it as a shared problem and both of you are now, presumably, looking for solutions to it instead of trying to defend opposing points of view.

Once you begin to look for the other person's point of view and play it back in your own words, your responses must become less automatic. You gain greater control of yourself and of the conversation. The conversation is no longer a battlefield, a contest of wills, a war, a debate, a quiz, a debriefing, a harangue, or a monologue. There are no scorekeepers and no scores. The conversation is also not a pretext for insulting or threatening anybody, nor is it a dumping ground for your problems.

If the single principle of the conversation is kept in mind, it is remarkably easy to decide what will, and what will not, make the conversation as good as it can be, as enriching in human values and potentials for further sharing. For example, the three R's of "rancor, remonstrance, and recrimination" are obviously inappropriate. Sweeping generalizations and a know-it-all attitude also tend to separate, rather than bring together, the parties. "Brain picking" produces resistance, and nobody is so subtle as to squeeze another's brain like a citrus fruit without the latter's noticing it. A series of idle questions is almost as objectionable and will have the other person reaching for the brake in short order.

If you need information, level with the other person and say so up front. Ask for permission; don't assume or pretend you're entitled to it; and be appreciative. Assessing blame and putting others on the defensive are not designed to make them more forthcoming. Enthusiasm and warmth, on the other hand, are virtually universal solvents for defensive walls.

Sharpening issues will not set the stage for cooperative efforts. Attempting to force or dominate the conversation is unmannerly and unproductive. Habitual advice-seeking and opinion-polling are also minuses, as are needless repetition and verbosity. Joe Louis nailed the latter flaw with this straight right: "A man that's got something to say don't need all week to make his point." Demanding, insisting, and interrupting all belong in the same column. Gloom and doom sharers are much too generous. And the booby prize for conversational maladroitness goes to those who consistently underestimate others and act accordingly.

On the other hand, there is a sense of propriety, of balance, of give and take, of sharing, in a good conversation. In order to get close enough to other people to touch and move them, you have to be willing to present yourself openly, but it is a mistake to volunteer too much too soon. Your entire curriculum vitae in one sitting is inappropriate, and it is more interesting if your background is solicited and gradually pieced together over the course of several conversations than if you spell it out in detail at your earliest opportunity. Give the relationship a chance to build and a sense of continuity. Let it grow at its own natural rate; don't try to force its growth by drowning it in autobiography.

Individual differences must be taken into account. Some people enjoy mealtime conversations best. Others are on a diet and would prefer almost any other setting. Some like to speak on the telephone in midafternoon; others have their own best times. When and where a particular person is most available to you can be learned if you are observant. But whenever and wherever it is, the conversation may be viewed as a meeting ground or playing field on which your willingness to look for opportunities to reduce separations and your goodwill and good spirits will create opportunities which did not previously exist.

There is another extremely important communications capability that should be mentioned here. Within each one of us, at a certain level of mind activity, is a powerful and

extremely useful but largely underutilized two-way communications system. Although many people are becoming aware of
the existence of this important message center, most still
needlessly deny themselves access to it.

In June, 1963, I read the surgeon general's report on the
effects of smoking and decided to give up the habit
permanently. I'd tried to do so several times before but had
never been able to stop smoking for more than a few days. I was
aware, in a general way, that if I gave up smoking, I might
"sublimate" this so-called oral need by overeating, become
obese, and succumb to cardiovascular diseases. However, the
possibility of carcinoma and metastasis and the other scary
clinical details I'd read about in the report seemed to be the
more immediate danger, particularly as I'd never been a pound
overweight in my life.

Having made this decision, I had no idea how to
implement it, but a friend told me he'd accomplished this
objective through self-hypnosis. My knowledge of self-
hypnosis was somewhat limited as it consisted largely of my
recollection of the contents of a five-cent "little blue book" on
the subject published by the Haldeman-Julius Company that
I'd sent away for when I was about ten. However, my friend
was kind enough to supplement this knowledge with the loan
of a dollar paperback, and I was soon ready to have a go at it.

I sat quietly in a chair and fixed my gaze at a point on the
opposite wall slightly above my horizontal line of sight and
took several relaxing deep breaths. Without more than the
slightest idea of what I was doing, I tried to "contact" my
"subconscious mind," as per the instructions. I began to give
myself "negative suggestions"; that is, I thought of all of the
negative consequences of smoking which might befall me. This
mental list included many diseases I was able to picture fairly
clearly from my recent reading of the surgeon general's report.
I thought of the bad taste in my mouth, the dangers of injury or
death in a fire caused by smoking in bed, the possible damage
to clothing and furniture, the nicotine stains on teeth and

fingers, the waste of money, etc. I suggested all of these possibilities for myself if I continued to smoke but concentrated, for the most part, on the various diseases I'd read about in the report.

I then began to give myself a series of "positive suggestions." I told myself how marvelous my health and well-being would become after I gave up this habit and mentally pictured myself as a happy, healthy, prosperous nonsmoker. The entire procedure might seem quite ludicrous but it is a fact I have never smoked anything from that day to this, have no desire to do so, and my weight has remained constant, give or take five pounds, over the period. This is, to be sure, merely anecdotal evidence and might easily be written off. On the other hand, I know many people who have kicked the smoking habit via almost the identical route, and the evidence keeps mounting.

At any rate, I didn't explore any of the other possibilities inherent in this procedure until I had the dream described in the first chapter of this book. It seemed clear to me this dream was intended as a message to myself from another level of my own mind. It was reasonable to theorize that there was a means of sending messages to another level of one's own mind and a means of receiving messages from another such level. I decided to do some further research.

Based on what I learned, it is my opinion that the most readily available and best route to the benefits inherent in reaching other levels of mind is José Silva's method, described in *The Silva Mind Control Method*, by José Silva and Philip Miele, a Pocket Book edition.

I impart the following with a certain amount of indebtedness to the Silva method and to a lecturer on this subject with whom I spoke. In sleep, we produce several different levels of brain-wave activity. A full cycle of all of the different levels of brain-wave activity takes place during about ninety minutes of sleep. One of these levels is called Alpha. Alpha is easily self-induced, and all of our dreams occur during this level. During the average night's sleep we go through about five full cycles, each of which contains an Alpha level. In each Alpha level of sleep, we have approximately three dreams. Thus, we have about fifteen dreams each night, but most people remember only one or two dreams or fragments, usually of the last dream they have before awakening. Most of this dream material is therefore lost to consciousness, and valuable clues to self-awareness are placed out of reach.

The Silva method teaches how to recover this material and how to use it to advantage. You may, for example, put yourself into Alpha before retiring and suggest you will awaken during the night or in the morning with a recollection of your dreams. You may then write down or tape-record a statement of your dreams, with the objective of interpreting them. Silva believes that dreams reflect experience, attitude, and concern. Because dreams reflect your own experience, your dream symbols often have particular, as opposed to universal, meaning, and you may therefore be the best interpreter of your own dreams, given the opportunity to do so.

The method also teaches how to obtain many other beneficial results. These include the ability to learn more quickly; to improve memory; ways to dream solutions to problems; the elimination of unwanted habits; the promotion of healing and other health benefits; and the production of additional advantages without drugs or hypnosis.

Perhaps one's mind is something like the third umpire in the following conversation among three Big League umpires:

"I call 'em as I see 'em," declared the first umpire.

"I call 'em as they are," rejoined the second umpire.

"Until I call 'em," insisted the third umpire, "they ain't nothin'."

If we are correct in assuming that our minds are of tremendous, even controlling, importance in our lives, it would be reasonable to suppose that a greater familiarity with and understanding and utilization of other levels of our mind than our everyday consciousness, levels ordinarily unexplored, would be of great interest and value.

All for one, one for all,
that is our device.

Alexandre Dumas
The Three Musketeers

Not Even Superman Works Alone

One of the milder replies I've heard from a stand-up comic to a heckler is: "Excuse me, sir (or madam). I don't need your help. I work alone." Despite appearances, he or she really doesn't. True, the comics are standing up there alone, and if they bomb, they're all alone, but if successful, they almost undoubtedly will have an agent and probably a personal manager, too. More than likely they will have a good deal-making lawyer on their team, as well as an accountant, maybe a business manager, and of course (or, almost of course) writers. This does not include a secretary, a road manager, traveling companions, a factotum or two, public relations people, and assorted members of their claque—all options of the very hot.

The self-made man or woman is virtually extinct. Batman, as you may recall, was only the senior member of a Dynamic Duo. He was also a close personal friend of the Gotham City police commissioner and had, in the chief of police and the entire law enforcement apparatus of that metropolis, staunch allies. In addition, he had great social contacts, a personal fortune, highly advanced hardware and a far-out tailor. Not even Superman works alone, and how far would the one musketeer have gotten?

The message is clear: If you want to bomb, you can do that all by yourself. Success, however, will come a lot more easily if you've got a good, strong team effort behind you. A "buddy system" of your own personal alliances will help you with almost any conceivable objective. The most obvious example is negotiating the jumps and hurdles of the corporate steeplechase.

For a brief period, I worked for a family-owned-and-operated business. I could appreciate that if the owner's son and I were vying for the same corporate slot, I'd probably get something else, but I was under the mistaken notion that similar rules didn't apply to large, publicly owned corporations. I thought all that was necessary was a darned good job well done and I'd rise to the level of my ability. I was wrong, and the fact this simple concept escaped my notice as long as it did cost me money and valuable career time. My career did advance, but not at the same rate as those who had inside help. What I didn't sufficiently take into account was that, while nepotism was only rarely the crucial factor in drafting important changes in the tables of organization of large, publicly traded corporations, a personal connection with those who had the power to implement the changes, or to influence them, was often decisive. Personal relationships were also, to be sure, "thicker than water." Interestingly, one of the nation's top corporate executives may have been brought down on both accounts. After Mr. Lee Iacocca was fired from the presidency of the Ford Motor Company, he was quoted as saying: "When I went to Ford thirty-two years ago, I knew it was a family empire. But it just never entered my mind that I could have a problem someday. I thought if I was the best, I'd be all right, dynasty or not."

The process of selection is more Darwinian than Machiavellian in its operation. Indeed, there is nothing sinister about it. If a small group of candidates for an important promotion contains one member known and liked by the person to make the selection, or if the latter feels relatively neutral toward the members of the group but one candidate has a strong advocate close to the decision-maker's ear, who is almost certain to be selected? Why not help a buddy if it's possible and it's thought he or she can handle the job? What are friends in court for?

Other things being fairly equal (which is always said to be the case when the choice narrows down to the friend or associate of the person with the power, or somebody close to him or her, and a couple of other candidates who might be a little better qualified), wouldn't most people want to have, and feel more comfortable near, somebody they know and like, somebody loyal and reliable, or at least somebody strongly recommended by a person whose judgment they trust, particularly if the promotion involves a key post? The choices made are almost never completely off the wall, and if a particular executive takes a bit longer to grow into a new position, bottom lines (net corporate profits) are usually unaffected. What more often happens is that the post loses some of its power but none of its salary, fringes, or perks.

The buddy system is not only at work in shifting the players already on the corporate game board, but it also operates to place new players (who are brought in from outside the company) in key squares. In fact, often the greatest opportunities lie with those who are thus able to make high, valuting leaps from outside the company into strong first positions. This is especially true when extremely favorable contracts are negotiated. Corporations are more easily induced to grant super deals to those their managements wish to lure away from their competitors than to those already part of the stable. But whether the promotion is made from within or without the company, it carries with it, in addition to all of its other rewards, increased visibility, thus setting the stage for future promotions, while those not so favored are doubly hampered. They remain in relative obscurity and do so at lesser incomes, fringes, perks, and power. On the one hand, nothing succeeds like success and bodies in motion tend to remain in motion; on the other, bodies at rest tend to remain at rest.

Visibility is of extreme importance and is almost always to be much preferred to a pay rise. The proper exposure is usually vital to almost any important objective. In corporate life, for example, it is the proximity to higher and higher levels of management within your own company, as well as to outside managements, that provides a direct route to executive sweets.

It is obvious that in a race among many entrants, a driver with a highly detailed and accurate map of the route to an unfamiliar destination several hundred miles away has an almost insurmountable advantage over other, equally good, drivers who are not sure how to get there. The map provides an overview of the terrain for the one who possesses it; the others must find their own way and there will, presumably, be much trial and error, much stopping along the way, a greater likelihood of mishap, and much delay. If any among the mapless arrive at the destination at all, they will be late and harried and their journey can hardly be expected to have been a joyride.

It should be no great surprise that winners usually have an overview of the terrain which gives them direct access to their objectives. Trying to find a way out of a tricky maze of ten-feet-high hedges, at ground level, may be a formidible task. However, given an overview of the maze at a height of even a few feet above the hedge tops, with the baffles and barriers put in perspective, the problem is easily solved. Looked at from this point of view, it is not the design and construction of the maze that presents the problem but the lack of the overview. Once the direct route becomes visible, the difficulties disappear and the path to freedom is clear.

Would it not be valuable, therefore, to spend some time acquiring the overview and the direct access which provide the most efficient route to what you want? Why continue to battle the maze of the particular circumstances in which you find yourself, on its own turf, spending your spiritual and material resources fruitlessly? To keep fighting the terrain at ground level is an abrading and lacerating process. It is also unnecessary, for you may be able to build a network of helpers that will enable you to finesse the detours and dead ends, the trials and errors, of those who continue to slug it out in the trenches year after year.

This approach is a little like playing rummy. Every single time a card is turned, you have an opportunity to improve your hand, and, as in rummy, if you fail to do so too often, you are assuring inevitable losses for yourself. The idea is to begin to build an environment in which you may flourish, to begin to create movement in a desired direction, to begin to develop this movement into a momentum that drives your venture forward. The operative word is "begin," for in this initial move you break the inertial forces binding you into a fixed position from which development is rendered impossible and you create a new and vital rhythm in your life that begins to vibrate like a tuning fork. These vibrations, these self-created emanations, pick up other, sympathetic vibrations in their proximity, and the first link in a new relationship is forged.

Let us assume the opening move involves an objective that is based either on a current interest of yours (something on which you may already have spent much time and thought) or on a hope or dream (something you'd like very much to become involved with but have put off for one or more reasons). To accomplish either objective, and to realize all of its benefits, will require an active approach.

While you are steeping your thoughts in the flow of benefits that will accrue to you through the realization of your plan (this optimistic mind-set is useful) and allowing your mind to become aware of the positive results in your life to be created, some active preparation is in order. No matter how esoteric your field of interest, be it even the knitting of glass hats, others are already involved in it, and some of them can and will be happy to help you if you properly present yourself to them.

You will, if you wish to do so, soon be moving among

people in your chosen field of interest, many of whom may presently be much better informed about the subject that surrounds, or is an integral part of, your objective. The fact that others with whom you will be associating know more than you in this regard should in no way intimidate you, for two principal reasons. First, the more others know about your subject, the better positions they will be in to help you, that is, the more valuable they will be when they join your team. Second, they will want to help you, not because of your knowledge or the lack of it, but because they like you and want to have you about.

However, to help guide your excursions to the best fishing waters, you will want to scout the area and get a better overview. It will be useful to begin to learn who the major players are and to get a better current background of the subject. I am here assuming you are not already an expert and have few, if any, contacts in the field.

A professional librarian at the largest public library accessible to you can be of immense help in getting you oriented. A single telephone call to a first-rate librarian—in which you solicit help in acquiring a list of books, periodicals, trade groups, organizations, societies, information offices, public relations companies, and any other referrals the librarian may know of that can supply further information and leads to potential personal contacts—will provide a good first pass at bridging the gaps.

A useful approach is to tell the person answering the library telephone that you are trying to get some help in your field of interest and that you were wondering whether there was at the library somebody particularly knowledgeable about that subject. If there is such a person, you may be able to get his or her name and you are halfway home. Whether or not there is such a person at that library (and you are not limited to only one library; in fact, if the subject lends itself, a college, university, or professional school library might be preferable), after stating the purpose of the call, you might follow with: "Would it be possible, Mr. or Ms. So-and-So, for you to suggest some starting points for getting a good perspective of the field and some current knowledge?"

The words "Would it be possible...?" are effective in most cases because the request is made in the form of a question, not a demand, there is a note of appeal in it, and an implication of a level of difficulty involved that tends to put the other person on his or her mettle; and laying in the other's name makes your appeal more personal.

As you begin to acquire a perspective and some current information (trade periodicals are helpful in the latter context), certain pieces of information will be of particular interest. Copy this material or clip it from a periodical if you own it and staple or tape it into a scrapbook. Include the names, titles, and affiliations of industry spokespeople, chief executive officers, and other prominent executives of companies in the field; if any of them is quoted as saying something you may find useful for any reason, by all means add this to your scrapbook. This simple technique will not only give you a better grasp of the subject matter, a better appreciation of who's who in the industry and with whom you feel some empathy, but over the course of time, a review of your scrapbook may reveal, illuminate, or target your own specific interests in the field. Should this happen, it will give you a more precise direction toward your objective.

While this information-gathering process is going on, join the professional or industry organizations available to you and become active in them. This will put you well on your way toward selecting and fielding your own team of helpers. Many of these organizations will probably require your being sponsored for membership. This is another service your scrapbook should provide.

First, request the membership forms in a telephone call. Don't ask any questions in this call that will reveal your own lack of knowledge; simply ask for the forms to be mailed to you. Read the membership application carefully. If you need the sponsorship of other members or professionals in the field, you may ask for the membership directory in the hope of finding sponsors you know or some people known to mutual friends or acquaintances, or you may refer to your scrapbook, if appropriate, and simply write to several of the people you select, soliciting their sponsorship of your membership application. State the fact that you took the liberty of seeking their help because you felt a rapport with them based upon (and here you quote from your scrapbook what you liked and cite its source). Many people will be happy to help you and will be flattered by the fact their statement has been remembered in this way. Provide a stamped, self-addressed envelope and any information they may need. Of course, you must acknowledge anybody who helps you in another letter and you may later thank them in person, too.

If you need a specific background and don't have it, ask the membership secretary whether it would be possible for you to substitute some other background which may be analogous. State your preparations and interest in becoming a member. Let it be known you have done some work to prepare for joining their organization. If you can enclose a personal recommendation from somebody known to the membership secretary, so much the better. State your enthusiasm and interest. If it is made possible for you to join, thank the membership secretary or the committee in writing.

If you are soliciting sponsorship and don't fully qualify but have been permitted to apply, be honest about your lack of qualifications and indicate that the membership secretary has been kind enough to allow you to apply for membership. Here you may quote from your letter in which you thanked the secretary. Although you may be mailing this letter to several people, you will be composing one basic letter, so spend a little time on it and get it worded to your satisfaction. Any help you may receive should be acknowledged and may provide a basis for a more personal relationship.

If there are several organizations you'd like to join, you will probably find some are easier for you to get into than others. Often, by joining the easier one(s) first, you may use these as a means of "bootstrapping" yourself into the more difficult ones. For example, the American Federation of Television and Radio Artists (AFTRA) is easier to join than is the Screen Actor's Guild (SAG). However, for many years, (although no longer the case) members of AFTRA might qualify for SAG simply because they were members of a "sister" union despite the fact they would otherwise fail to qualify.

As a member of these organizations, you gain direct, face-to-face contact with successful men and women in the field. By becoming an active member, you not only attend luncheons, dinners, and other meetings but you have an opportunity to volunteer to serve on many committees and develop close working relationships with many people who may be prospective members of your own personal success team. The time you contribute may be viewed as a form of dues-paying, but the benefits far outweigh the costs.

In addition to scope for broadening your base of knowledge and personal contacts, these organizations offer a number of other fringe benefits to their members. They will probably offer a library or other informational source, as well as free professional advice as to how best to pursue your interest. Group life and health insurance are usually available through this kind of association. Sometimes, individuals who may need such coverage badly are not eligible for it. As a member of a group such as this, even individually uninsurable risks may be accepted. Those who would normally be insurable on their own may find they receive better coverage and at a lower cost in this way. You will also probably have access to a membership directory and much biographical information about the membership that will give you leads as to how to approach some of them later. Discounts on industry-connected books and periodicals, on car rentals, and on big-ticket items, such as major appliances and automobiles, are often available, as are group travel opportunities and seminars. Many of these extras offer additional means of both broadening your base of knowledge and your personal contacts. A credit union is also a fairly standard adjunct to many industry organizations. This usually allows you to save money at slightly higher rates or to borrow money at slightly lower rates of interest than otherwise available. Of course, if one or more of these benefits are not available, you may initiate action through existing channels to create them. The annual dues for all of this are modest.

It is advisable to take advantage of every possibility to convert your uncommitted time into knowledge and personal contacts, with the emphasis on the latter. If you spend some time with the other members, you may expect to receive invitations. One common invitation is a vaguely worded expression of interest in having lunch. Such invitations usually remain in limbo; neither party makes the follow-up call. You should show some initiative. At the time the invitation is extended, demonstrate some enthusiasm in acknowledging it: "Great idea, Fred (or Sally). I'm going to call you early next week to firm it up." If, when you call, the other party backs away from having lunch with you, leave the door open but don't press. Suggest the other person call you when his or her schedule is more definite. Above all, don't take it as a personal slight. No harm's done and nothing is lost. When you see the other person again, be as cordial as always.

Should the luncheon take place, be upbeat, optimistic, enthusiastic, pleasant, and keep it light. This is not the time to go heavily into your autobiography. Do not ask lots of questions. You want to be friendly and casual. If questions arise as to your background in the field, state the fact that you're tremendously interested in the field, although your own contribution to it has been rather limited so far. If help is volunteered, express your great appreciation but don't ask for help, directly or indirectly.

As we saw in an earlier chapter, people like to do business with and have about them those people whose company they enjoy. This is the kind of favorable impression you should be making, and it's not really difficult to do this. Avoid the negative. If the food is not prepared precisely as you ordered it, don't complain about it. If you ordered broccoli and an endive salad and you receive zucchini and mixed greens, unless you're

executives, and public speakers. You, however, do not want to keep people at a distance, and bright colors will make you more accessible, more easily approached.

Try to look good. Be aware of your posture, voice tones, and facial expressions. Your clothes should be clean and well pressed, and you should be well groomed. A small sum paid to a first-rate hairdresser or barber who can style your hair professionally is a recommended expenditure.

Some of the people with whom you establish a rapport will begin to take an interest in you, and they may volunteer to help you in unexpected ways. For example, a woman I know was doing some volunteer work in connection with an organization she'd joined. A man on the same committee, whom she'd met briefly at a meeting some weeks earlier, learned, on inquiry, that she owned and operated an employment agency. He volunteered to introduce her to a friend who was one of the largest employers in that part of the country. The introduction resulted in a considerable and continuing source of income for the woman.

Meeting new people in this way can be an adventure. As you develop your personal relationships with the people you find congenial, you will be associating with them in different settings. You will want to meet with them outside of the auspices of the organization that brought you into initial contact. You will want to visit with each other in your residences. You may have other social, recreational, or business interests in common to share. These shared activities will broaden and deepen the relationship. You and your new friend or acquaintance know many other people, and you may wish to introduce one another to some of them. Don't overlook the possibility that there may be other ways for you and your friend to share in mutually profitable ventures that lie outside the field of the organization at which you met.

An additional opportunity may lie in forming a small group of people either within the original field of interest that brought you into contact with your new associates or not, as you choose. A monthly dinner meeting of this group, for the purpose of sparking ideas off one another, can produce beneficial results for all. Whether the group is within the original field or not, it should contain people of varied skills and areas of expertise.

All intelligent people have ideas, but unless they are executed, they remain in filing cabinets and closets. A group such as this provides a synergy and a mix of expertise that can breathe life into an idea. Someone in the group may know of others who can be of further help in executing projects set in motion by the group.

A thorough understanding of the basic principles and their implementation will create marvelous opportunities for you. The active approach multiplies the possibilities. Your skills in personal relationships and communication will convert several of these possibilities to realities. As these conversions enter your life, you cannot help but become enriched, both materially and spiritually. As you get behind the wheel of your own life and take the controls, you will feel better about yourself. As this feeling is communicated and shared, you begin to draw into your life precisely what you need to keep you functioning at a happy and creative level. It is both unnecessary and unsatisfactory to be the one musketeer fighting the world. So, put some good people on your team. Enroll others and discover how much more fun it is to play the game.

Looking Good

Although the use of such nicknames as Fatso, Shorty, Skinny, Runt, and the like are slowly receding in popularity in our urban population centers, how people look (and sound and smell) affects the way others think of them and how others react to them. You and I might deny these effects on ourselves, of course. We don't ordinarily like to admit that our judgments of others are based on such superficial sensory data. Only other people do that. But, somehow, those who appeal to our senses (the media have exerted a strong conditioning effect in this regard) attract and influence us disproportionately, and we would have to be other than human if we remained neutral to the myriad bits of data we receive every day.

How we present ourselves says something about us. The package of sensory data we transmit becomes a kind of medium by which others continually read us. It is as if the book which is the self, the person, the inner being, is, indeed, judged by its cover, the sum of the data revealed by the outer self. Others perceive these data and react accordingly.

Neither you nor I would buy a used car from certain people. Others interest and attract us at once. It is instructive to observe how talented professionals convey character in dramatic presentations. Acting, lighting, makeup, wardrobe, props, direction are all parts of the composite, and there are many additional pieces that mesh and interlock to create the covering by which we have learned to judge the contents. It is also worth studying how candidates for elective office present themselves. What they say and how they look when they deliver their pitch must be of a piece, for if we are jarred by a sense of a lack of synchronization between the words and the picture, we will be put off.

The Scottish poet Robert Burns, in "To a Louse," wrote:

Oh wad some power the giftie gie us
To see oursels as others see us!
It wad frae monie a blunder free us,
    An' foolish notion.

The sentiments expressed are as accurate today as when committed to paper about two hundred years ago. Despite the billions of dollars and hours spent each year in this country on how we look, most people really don't know what kind of image they present. There seems to be a gentleman's agreement to perpetuate this ignorance. Nobody, for example, is likely to approach you on the street or over cocktails and tell you that the suit you're wearing doesn't fit or that your hair looks ridiculous. You are far more likely to hear repeated confirmations that you look great or terrific. It is easy to understand that with reinforcement like this, there is little incentive for change.

Notwithstanding much complacency, there is enormous room for improvement in the way most of us present ourselves and in the quality of the self-awareness of the image we project. We may, if we wish, present an image of ourselves that works for us, that is a valuable asset. If we are willing to make the effort, we may rewrite our message.

Beginning at the top, my guess is that at least three out of four people fail to style their hair in a way that contributes most to their appearance. It was not until my first television appearance that I realized I had been one of the three out of four all of my life. The day after the program aired, which was the kickoff of the publicity campaign on my first book, I received a letter from the publisher criticizing the fact that my hair looked plastered down. I was told I looked like a used car salesman. Some of my friends had additional unflattering comments. In fact, my own barber, who had, by coincidence seen the program, told me that his wife had chided *him* for the way *I* looked.

The comments were apt. I had failed to see myself as the television cameras saw me and as successive segments of the public would see me. The greasy-kid-stuff-wet-look made me appear insincere, and the impact of what I was trying to accomplish was undercut in a nationally syndicated telecast.

It has been widely speculated that the physical appearance of Messrs. Kennedy and Nixon in their televised debates determined the outcome of the 1960 presidential election. Marshall McLuhan pointed out that "TV would inevitably be a disaster for a sharp, intense image like Nixon's, and a boon for the blurry, shaggy texture of Kennedy." Professor McLuhan, in differentiating media and explaining what works effectively in the various media, tells us that the television image is of low intensity or definition, unlike movies, and gives us a lack of detailed information about objects. Visually low in data, the television image gives the viewer approximately three million dots per second, from which, Professor McLuhan tells us, the viewer accepts only several dozen each instant from which to make an image. The viewer's intensity of involvement derives from his or her participation in creating an image from among a mosaic of dots.

"Anybody who looks as if he might be a teacher, a doctor, a businessman, or any of a dozen other things all at the same time is right for TV," says McLuhan. "When the person presented *looks* classifiable, as Nixon did, the TV viewer has nothing to fill in. He feels uncomfortable with this TV image.

He says uneasily, 'There's something about this guy that isn't right.'" Jimmy Carter's television style would appear to be particularly effective. His White House telecast in a sweater, the paid political television announcements in jeans, his blurry, fuzzy, undefined, non-hard-edged image are all well suited to television. His imprecision is actually an asset in this all-important medium.

It is reasonable to expect that as the phenomenal penetration of television reorients the thinking patterns of a society, what is an effective presentation of the self on television will become the standard for what works in everyday life. Not only will more emphasis be placed on the visual, the appearance, the look you and I project, but the specifics of what is effective will be directly carried over from the television medium into the culture.

In considering how the way we look affects others, it might help create some objectivity if we thought of ourselves as ambulatory pieces of sculpture. From that point of view, does the way you look make a statement about you, and if so, what is the statement? What thoughts and feelings does your appearance evoke in other people?

The greatest single change you can make in your personal look and one of the least expensive, is your hairstyle. There is not an appreciable difference in price, in most cases, between what you now pay to have your hair cut and what it would cost for the services of somebody excellent to create a style that even an average haircutter could later duplicate. As in the case of designer dresses and suits, the creation is the valuable contribution. Copying the style is no great trick, and the copies properly sell at a small fraction of the price of the originals. Get advice from a competent professional. If you're not pleased with the result, when your hair needs recutting, get another opinion. Once you find a pro with whom you are satisfied, be open to his or her advice on other aspects of how your hair can look its best for you. If this advice isn't forthcoming, ask for it and acknowledge it with words and money.

If you cannot find a satisfactory haircutter, one who can

help you decide on a look that's right for you, you might consider this approach: Most readers of this book who reside in this country will probably find themselves close enough to one or more local television stations. Study your local television newscasters, reporters, weather and sports people, and talk-show hosts and hostesses. Find a hairstyle you like, preferably one you think would work for you; however, even if the style would not work for you, if it works especially well for the on-camera person you have selected, you're looking at the result of hairstyling talent that can also be put to work for you.

Call the station and ask that person's secretary for the name and address of the talent's hair stylist. With a little persistence and ingenuity you will have a viable starting point toward remodeling your image into a work of art that makes a statement you'd like to hear about yourself instead of the message you're currently sending out. Be willing to try two or three different approaches. If the secretary won't tell you, call the television personality. If that doesn't work, call the makeup department of the station and ask them. If you keep trying, you should be able to get this information.

If there is a local on-camera television person who is turned out in clothing that appeals to you and you think similar styles would work for you, you might try the same approach. I mention local talent first because they will probably be stylishly dressed in ways acceptable in the particular region in which you live and they probably shop locally, so that the problem of creating a similar image for yourself is simplified. However, you may also want to consider national talent. In the case of entertainment programming, there will probably be a credit line at the end of the program that indicates where at least some of the clothing was gotten.

If you can find an on-camera person whose style you like and with whom you share basic physical characteristics such as height, weight, coloring, age, you may be more certain that what works for this person will work for you and you may study him or her to your advantage on a color television set. However, you should be willing to experiment even if the similarities are not so pronounced between this person and yourself if you like the look sufficiently.

Study the person. It's not going to cost you anything, and you can learn a great deal. Time and talent went into creating this look; it didn't happen by itself no matter how casual it looks. In addition to hairstyle, become aware of facial expressions, wardrobe, gestures, diction, voice tones, walk, posture. All of these variables can be learned, and you can begin these observations on your own today. If you're ready for it, in many of the largest cities in the country you can find a professional who coaches people for television appearances and buy an hour of his or her time. You will be able to see yourself on video tape and hear some objective, informed comments that could be of great value. Don't spend hundreds of dollars an hour; the cost shouldn't exceed that of a good dinner in the same city.

Before continuing, those readers who, for one reason or another, may find some of this material inappropriate, should be acknowledged. For example, some bald people (or others) may be put off by my beginning with hairstyling. Others may object to other parts of this chapter. Some with physical disabilities may find some parts inapplicable. I apologize to these people (and others who may object) and ask their indulgence. I would say, in passing, that many people with physical disabilities have exhibited great style and that a disability in one or more areas need not preclude improving one's presentation to the best of one's abilities. President Franklin Roosevelt, for example, had a gift for speaking, a strong dramatic sense, and a flair for clothes.

The next variable, omitting surgery as outside the scope of this material, is teeth. How many movie or television stars can you name who have crooked or chipped teeth or large spaces between their teeth or stained or loose or missing teeth? Some may object on the grounds that the film and television industries place too much emphasis on physical appearance and that such standards are superficial or meaningless.

First, there is a medical argument that can be made in

terms of the health benefits for those with straight, clean, well-aligned, strong, good teeth. They are able to chew and digest food more efficiently; their teeth better support one another and the chances for permanence of their teeth are improved. In addition, there is some support for the contention that how you look mirrors who you are. After the age of forty, it has been said, you get the face you deserve.

There is also an esthetic argument that can be advanced, but these and other arguments, both pro and con, need not detain us here. In this context, I am only attempting to suggest what works best for most people. I am not for a moment attempting to justify the observation that attractive people fare better in this world. It is fairly clear that a better presentation of the self is self-enhancing. You and I may, if we wish, create a set of conditions for ourselves in which we may thrive, or at least do better.

To stay with the subject of teeth, if you wanted to become a movie star, how your teeth looked would be considered. If they were unattractive, this would be communicated to you and you would be requested to take certain remedial action. The fact that in your present occupation or avocation or role nobody has made a similar request of you does not mean that if your teeth are noticeably imperfect, they are not working against your interests. How your teeth look is one index by which you are judged by others, again, for better or worse. It is something like the difference between your taking out a nineteen cent ballpoint or an expensive fountain pen. People notice the difference and make judgments accordingly. This would not necessarily be the case in a world of philosophers, but it is a practical reality. You would be hard pressed to compile not only a list of movie or television stars with noticeably imperfect teeth, but such a list of successful people in any field you'd care to name.

Attractive teeth are also an integral part of an attractive smile. Those with unattractive teeth have smiles which are less compelling, and they tend to smile less frequently and less naturally. Their facial expressions seem more forced and stiff, and this, too, is communicated. The effects are subtle but cumulative. Taken together, the net is to create discernible separations between these people and others.

Orthodontia, cumbersome and relatively unusual only a generation or two ago, was itself a source of real, if temporary, social discomfort and separation. However, technological improvements and a surge in popularity have combined to transform this procedure into a minor inconvenience. Not only young people, but adults in growing numbers, are flocking to specialists all across the country for this corrective treatment. The benefits in most cases begin to flow sooner than expected, for, when others become aware of your commitment to yourself, your stock rises with them. Significantly, your failure to make this commitment is equally obvious, and your apparent acceptance of a defect or deficiency of long standing is noted. Some observers may even begin to draw conclusions adverse to your interests as to why this condition was not remedied in your childhood. The benefits and detriments in this regard are obviously long-term.

Although my personal bias is toward the natural, nature is not always omniscient, or even kind. Art and science can combine to produce remarkable transformations, with human happiness and productivity the resultant by-products. Severely burned people and others badly injured in automobile and industrial accidents have been transformed by teams of dedicated professionals. In a less dramatic instance, after some testing, a man I know, who was extraordinarily short as a young child and teen-ager, underwent a series of treatments that stimulated his growth. He is about six feet tall today, handsome and outgoing. The last time I saw him he was being interviewed on "The David Susskind Show," and he looked great.

There are thousands of individual cases in which highly skilled professionals have combined their talents to produce almost miraculous results. These cases are cited, in passing, because while they are beyond the scope of this book, they are illustrative of what can be done. We may expect great progress and even more dramatic results in pharmacology, endocrinology, and other medical specialties, including genetic reprogramming and bionic replacements. The "six million dollar man" and the "bionic woman" will undoubtedly spawn real progeny.

Those who simply want to present themselves more effectively have a relatively easy task. Cosmetic acupuncture, a treatment that dates back almost five thousand years in China, is beginning to catch on in this country. Although many acupuncturists do not believe in or practice cosmetic acupuncture, its proponents claim the advantages of a face-lift at a fraction of the cost and without the pain, scars, hospitalization, and other disadvantages of plastic surgery. The number of approximately half-hour treatments required depends upon variables such as the condition of the patient and his or her response. A dozen treatments might be about average.

The treatments are said to increase the circulation of blood to the face, to tighten and tone the skin, and to promote wrinkle-dispelling moisture. Some enthusiastic patients also report other beneficial results all over their body. Although the jury is still out on many of these claims, the down side for most medically screened patients would appear to be limited.

Anybody interested in this form of treatment would be well advised to thoroughly check the credentials of the practitioner and to avoid those whose backgrounds do not pass strict scrutiny. Most of the cosmetic acupuncture treatments given in this country to date have been administered by doctors in southern California and New York City.

The face is such an obvious focus of attention that anything that can be done to improve its look must make an important contribution to how others receive you. Relaxed facial expressions are attractive. Tense, clenched mouths, darting or shifting eyes, and other manifestations of stress put people off. Frowns, pouts, expressions of worry, consternation, disapproval, and the like are unattractive. These expressions not only create separations, but their habitual use tends to line and mark the face in ways that call attention to these negative characteristics even when such faces are in repose or are actually expressing approval.

A relaxed face also makes it easier to smile, which is a most attractive expression and one that requires the use of fewer muscles and less energy than it takes to look tense or nervous. A serene, relaxed look, particularly if combined with good posture and carriage and a good complexion, cannot fail to make you look more attractive. This is all part of the look of confidence, of self-assurance, of super ability. Some have it even under intense pressure; others cannot buy it.

There are a couple of relatively inexpensive products that can make a difference in the way you look and feel. The first is by far the best hairdressing I've ever used. Mike Douglas' barber in Philadelphia sold it to me, and it's great. It's called RK Hair Dressing Gel, and it's acid-balanced. The one I use is formulated for men, but they have products for women, too. This product so impressed me that I called the company, Redkin Laboratories, Inc., in Canoga Park, California, to find out where I could buy some in New York. I was asked for my zip code and given some stores nearby that stocked their products. At the same time, they recommended I try their RK Men's Bar, an organic cleanser, which I did. It's terrific, and there is a comparable women's product.

The Men's Bar contains wheat and protein in a mildly acidic base; allantoin, a compound of natural herb derivatives, has also been added. All soaps, even those containing lanolin, glycerine, and cold cream, are alkaline and their use upsets the protective acid mantle of healthy skin, causing a loss of its moisture balance and increasing the potential for skin problems. The basic formula of the cleanser (both men's and women's) has a pH of 5.5, and it was first used to help heal infant skin rash. The pH of all the products you use may be easily tested with Nitrazine papers made by the E. R. Squibb Company and generally available at pharmacies.

Needless to say, I have no connection with the company and no financial interest of any kind in it. The hairdressing costs about two dollars, the Men's Bar and its counterpart for women were $2.15 each for the three-ounce size.

The subject of facial hair should be considered. Extremes are ordinarily best avoided. In this regard, as in the definition of obscenity, the guide is usually contemporary community standards and your own good taste. When, for example, long sideburns were in vogue among men, fashionable length, width, and thickness denoted youthfulness, masculinity, vitality, virility. However, even the slightest extension beyond what was considered fashionable was seen as an exaggeration and subjected those so adorned to suspicion of defensiveness and cover-up.

Beards and moustaches, long popular among the academic community, evidenced an uptrend in the sixties and early seventies, particularly among the under-thirty age group, from whom it spread into the mainstream. This trend has been reversed. Beginning about the time the United States completed its military withdrawal from Vietnam, beards and moustaches were being shorn and men's hair, as well as their sideburns, were being cut shorter. A cleaner look was in. More difficult to solve is the problem of eliminating other kinds of undesirable or unattractive facial hair growth, which may require qualified professional help.

Fashion trends are less important than a sense of personal style. What goes well with your own physical look and what makes you feel good should be given primary attention. Short, heavy women, for example, will exaggerate these characteristics by wearing clothing that breaks the line of their body. A sash or belt will break the line, as will a color contrast, particularly at the waist. Large patterns will also emphasize shortness and bulkiness.

The texture of clothing is another consideration. The more textured fabrics—such as tweeds, bulky knits, velvets, corduroys, suedes—arouse a need for tactile fulfillment, perhaps on the same theory that McLuhan advances for our need to fill in the gaps of the television image. We want to get closer to those who wear these fabrics.

Clothing serves many functions, and the acquisition and maintenance of a wardrobe that works for you requires and deserves effort. Regional variations in climate will dictate, to some extent, fabric weights and even colors. Warm climates will require lighter-weight clothing and lighter, brighter colors. My personal preferences lean toward wool, cotton, linen, silk, and other natural fibers.

In men's suits, wool is the best material. It is more expensive than most other suiting material, but it can be tailored to fit better and it lasts longer. In many stores, when you buy an expensive suit, it's possible to extend its useful life and thereby reduce its relative cost by having a second pair of pants cut to your order, even if the suit is not custom-made.

The most expensive items in your wardrobe should be given ample shopping time. It makes little sense to rush the purchase of clothes that cost a lot of money. If you're buying a suit, or an expensive dress, for example, fit is extremely important and you should be courteously demanding of the tailor or fitter. By making some telephone calls in advance, you may easily learn the names of the head fitters or best tailors in the stores you patronize, and you should make sure this person is working on the premises on the days you intend to avail yourself of his or her services. Some of these people are out to lunch at odd hours so this should be checked, too. The best advice and service will thus be available to you at no extra charge, but you should be willing to tip this person and consider it a small sum well spent. Not to take advantage of this opportunity is akin to eating in the best restaurant in town on the chef's day off.

Timing your purchases to take advantage of sales can bring down the cost of your wardrobe. Staples like shoes, socks, stockings, underwear, pajamas, slippers, handkerchiefs, some ties, scarves, purses, and belts may easily be bought at sale prices. Higher-priced items are often available in a surprising range of price, depending upon when and where you buy them. If you care to learn about labels and suppliers and seek out real sales and legitimate discount stores, you can save a considerable percentage of the cost of looking good in quality clothing. If in doubt, I would suggest the reliable stores and shops convenient to you at sale times.

When making any clothing purchase, particularly the more costly ones, try to visualize how the purchase will fit into your total wardrobe and complement it. If it simply duplicates an item you already own, you might be better served with something else. Focus on the total look. If you're happy with the suit or dress you've picked out, be prepared to set it off with the right accessories. Most men's suits will almost always look attractive with a lighter-color shirt and a tie darker than the shirt.

If the right accessories are not already part of your wardrobe, don't make the mistake of wearing a great suit or dress with the wrong shoes, shirts or blouses. The total effect will be destroyed, and you will be demonstrating that you either don't know how to dress, have poor taste, or couldn't afford to buy the proper accessories. If the suit or dress is right and you want it, buy it. If the right accoutrements strain your budget to the breaking point either with cash or on credit, don't wear the item until you have the elements to create a total look that works for you.

On the subject of money, you've probably had the experience of squandering sums of it on clothes you weren't sure you wanted at the time you bought them. You'd left home with the objective of buying a suit, dress or coat and spent half a day looking and trying on until you were tired and hungry. You allowed yourself to settle for something not quite right, if only to avoid another day of fruitless looking. This is always a mistake.

Or, you may have come upon what would have been a great bargain if you wanted the item, which you didn't, but you allowed yourself to become persuaded. You bought it but you rarely wear it. After a decent interval, it was donated to charity, stuffed into a drawer you rarely open, or hung in a corner of the closet. This sort of self-indulgence is a needless waste and should be controlled.

On the other hand, what may seem to be an extravagance may actually be the best bargain. I once bought a simple solid-color, crew neck, wool ski sweater that cost about as much as I was spending for suits at the time, but I loved it. The moment I tried it on, I knew I had to buy it. That was twenty-two years ago, and I still like the feeling it gives me when I wear it. Good, properly fitting clothes not only make you look and feel good, but they also wear well, particularly if you take care of them. About a year ago, I spent more than one hundred fifty dollars for a ready-made pair of shoes. They were expensive, but they'll probably be serviceable for twenty years.

How you spend money is a personal choice. I prefer a great shirt or sweater to a bad dinner in an overpriced restaurant, but if the shirt or sweater were less than satisfactory, I might prefer a good meal or something else, or I might be content to wait until I could buy something that truly pleased me, even if it were a gift.

During the discussions and negotiations at Camp David that led to the Begin-Carter-Sadat agreements, an effective news blackout was maintained. Perhaps because there were so many reporters and so little news to report, the fact that Israeli Defense Minister Weizman liked President Sadat's cologne was widely publicized (it was Aramis). Women have been aware of the power of perfumes and body lotions for centuries. At prices that at least match that of gold, some of the world's ultrachic are having their own individual scents created and bottled.

Good men's colognes are moving up smartly in price but are still available at about the per ounce price of liquor in a fashionable metropolitan bar or restaurant. I've noticed that some of the best imported men's colognes are not the same products as are sold in the country of origin. The oils are imported, but the product is compounded in this country. This fact is usually divulged in an almost unreadably small type-size conveniently located on the underside of the bottle, and the notice may be removed from the sample bottle.

If you prefer the real stuff, as I do, or at least want to have the opportunity of making up your own mind, the duty-free shops at international airports have it. However, these shops won't sell their duty-free products (even if you're willing to pay the duty) to anybody without a ticket to a destination out of the country, and they arrange to have the purchase placed on board for you. My best courier is my daughter. Or, you may prefer to get from the local manufacturer an address of a place in the country of origin from whence you may arrange to have your purchases mailed directly to you. Whatever cologne you use, remember that "less is more." Even the best colognes are objectionable if splashed on too lavishly.

The sound of your voice is an important element in your total presentation. It's difficult to judge the quality of your own speech because you and I don't hear ourselves as others hear us. However, if you don't think your speech adequately represents you, a tape recorder may help in this connection. I also recommend some professional coaching. Ordinarily, I would guess that about one reader in a thousand would seriously consider hiring outside help to improve his or her voice tone, diction, phrasing, intonation, and the like. I've heard the extraordinary difference a little coaching and practice has made in the case of professional radio and television people. I would therefore urge those who might otherwise summarily dismiss this suggestion to remember the line from the old song: "It ain't hut ya say but the way hut ya say it." I'm not suggesting a long and expensive course of training. There are coaches available who work with radio and television people and business people who have to do a certain amount of public speaking. For about twenty dollars per hour, you should be able, perhaps with the help of your local radio or television station or through one of the talent unions like the American Federation of Television and Radio Artists (AFTRA), to find a coach who can help you.

As we enter the more elegant eighties, good grooming is again a big plus. "Clean" is respectable again. How we present ourselves is registering with a surprisingly tight cluster of responses from a broad cross section. Looking good is an asset almost anybody can claim with a little conscious effort.

> The great man is he
> who does not lose his childlike heart.
>
> *Mencius*

Playfulness

Children can teach us a great deal about playfulness, but we have to be willing to learn. They are great improvisers and don't have to make appointments to play. They respond to playfulness instinctively and immediately. There is no holding back. They can take a few scraps of wood and some discarded material and transform them into a flying boat. We, lost in the directions of an elaborate toy, are left far behind as the imaginative child creates a better plaything out of the box and the packing than the toy itself.

The joy and wonder of a child's world can once again be ours, but we have to be open to it. Too often a child's playfulness is not only not prized by adults, it is actively discouraged. I once heard a nursery school teacher tell a parent her son was immature. Turned out the child was four and a half.

Our daughter attended an excellent school in New York from nursery school through the eighth grade. The director of the school was and is a marvelous, spirited woman whose Ph.D. never got in the way of her rapport with the children.

However, not all of the teachers were always so finely tuned to the children's wavelengths.

One year, during an evening in which the parents were invited to visit the school and chat with their child's teachers, I waited my turn on the various lines at discreet distances from successive, brief, parent-teacher conferences. When I was told our daughter was doing well but "she likes to play," I wasn't sure how to respond. "Doing well *but* she likes to play." I was somewhat perplexed by the disjunctive form in which the information had been imparted and by the grave mien.

Had I been told she was doing well *and* she liked to play, I would have understood at once. Apparently a young child who liked to play was somehow being put in the wrong. Caught off guard, and with a growing line of waiting parents, I mishandled the response. I considered the report briefly and left without dissent. When another teacher gravely informed me that "Leslie likes to play," I'd had time to consider what I might have said the first time. "So do I," I replied with a broad smile.

The word "play" has many meanings. Play may involve engaging in zero sum games and sports in which winners win at losers' expense. It may involve simulating or dissembling. It may refer to gambling compulsively or discharging hostilities and tensions not harmlessly but in ways that result in homicide and suicide. Play may have a dozen or more other meanings and references, all of which put the player at odds with his or her environment, pit the player against the world (or part of it), and produce no joy.

Ah, but *playfulness* is something quite different, a truly wonderful sight to behold, a delightful activity in which to engage. Playfulness involves a willingness to enjoy oneself; it is exquisitely centered and has, ideally, no purpose other than itself. A playful nature puts you in context with what's wholesome and healing and pure and loving and supportive within yourself and others. It is harder to imagine a loving relationship between and among human beings devoid of playfulness than it is to imagine combustion without fuel.

There is an innocent, almost conspiratorial, intimacy in playful activity.

Playfulness is natural and instinctive among the young of the animal kingdom. Pups, cubs, kittens, even civilized children exhibit a playful nature. Too many such children, however, fail to retain their unsophisticated ability to be playful. All too early they "put away childish things," trading away the nourishing delights of playfulness for the "benefits" of play, short-changing themselves in an unnecessary reversal of Gresham's law.

Although it is difficult, it is not impossible to be playful while playing. The test is simple: If the playing is done for any value other than the playing itself, the playfulness is somewhere else. If you play golf, for example, in order to sell more insurance or real estate, you may be playing, but without playfulness. If you play for the exercise, for the purpose of improving your game, in order to win, for the release of frustration or aggression obtained by cracking the ball with a lethal weapon, or for any of myriad other reasons, playfulness is absent. If, however, while out playing golf, you happen upon a stray child, puppy, or kitten and engage her, him, or it in aimless play (none of these is a likely insurance prospect), you may well be experiencing playfulness.

Most games and sports, even if not played for any stated objective and not scored, are usually too highly structured to permit playfulness. Several forward-looking individuals are experimenting with a kind of play that is cooperative instead of competitive. The idea is to substitute "no-win" games and sports for the more usual such activities. A version of no-win volleyball has as its objective to keep the ball from hitting the ground; that is, to keep the game going instead of trying to spike the ball into an opponent or otherwise score points.

The score becomes secondary or of even less importance. Often the game is not scored at all. The weaker players are encouraged to play because they are not put uptight about hurting their team's chances of winning. There is nothing to win in the usual sense. Everybody wins because everybody plays and enjoys the freedom of participating in this way.

It is easy to dismiss the genuine importance of playfulness. Our Puritan forefathers were convinced that the Devil would find work for "idle" hands. Kite-flying and snorkeling would have been about as unthinkable for Cotton Mather or Jonathan Edwards as disco dancing or surfing or playing with a frisbee to some of our more sober citizens today.

For those who must find a "useful" reason for everything they do, perhaps the words of Konrad Lorenz may be persuasive: "All the data of natural science, which are responsible for Man's domination of the world, originated in activities that were indulged in exclusively for the sake of amusement. When Benjamin Franklin drew sparks from the tail of his kite he was thinking as little of the lightning conductor as Hertz when he investigated electrical waves was thinking of radio transmission." Nor did any of the participants dream the Battle of Waterloo would be "won on the playing fields of Eton."

From another point of view, however "useful" the by-products of playfulness may prove to be, there is a joy, a purity, a frolicsomeness, a freedom, a merriness about playful activity that gives it zest and makes it fun. For these reasons alone, it is a most welcome pursuit; no other justifications are needed. Playfulness provides an improved alignment with humanity for those who indulge in it.

Dr. Karl Menninger (with Martin Mayman and Paul Pruyser) writes in *The Vital Balance: The Life Processes in Mental Health and Illness* (Viking Press): Love in its modifying function determines those essential ways of life which we call work and play.... Play likewise, seems to be very easy and rewarding for some, very difficult for others. These variations are important, since most of our treatment program depends upon their exploitation and development. More important than either play itself or work itself is the balance [an ever recurring word in this book] which is established between the two." At an absolute minimum, playfulness helps to provide this vital balance.

Like play, playfulness may be solitary (snorkeling), associative (surfing), and cooperative (frisbee). The context for playfulness, however, is not so structured as that of play. There is much room for improvisation in playful activity. There is no script or it is soon thrown away. The playful moment is fresh and free. It is more like jazz than symphony, more like rallying than playing a set, more like a Fellini movie than a Hitchcock. It finds its content in the moment, and it is flexible enough to incorporate whatever it will in and of the moment. It is open to the unexpected, to surprise, and it is not competitive. Scorekeeping is unimportant. It is natural and often occurs in a natural setting. In its aliveness to the moment it is creative as well as recreative.

The sometimes overly serious competition of Little League ball has been considered from the point of view of its damaging effects on children. Children have been known to weep bitterly at the loss of a game and to brood about their own errors, sometimes for weeks. Having to perform before a crowd of spectators is also a strain that is unnecessary and undesirable for young children. Recently I read a front-page headline in the New York *Daily News* that cited several permanent injuries sustained by children who had been competing in a tug-of-war. Even the name of the game has an unpleasant connotation. Several years ago I met a fellow on the beach who had been a pitcher on his college baseball team. After a fielding error by one of his teammates cost their side the game, this man walked over to the hapless fellow and punched him in the face.

Competitive sports reinforce the tendency to be highly competitive in school, in business, in social life, and even in close personal relationships. They are based on bad ecology and a scarcity mentality that drives people to take care of number one at all times for fear of there not being enough of whatever it is to go 'round. The growing minority who operate from an abundance point of view are aware that there need be no shortage. They have discovered that when you give trust, compassion, sincerity, cooperation, or love, you are likely to receive what you gave and are never without.

Playfulness is often actively discouraged in our society. Work is encouraged to the point that it threatens to eliminate true play. And work, as we all know, must be hard. The supreme distortion or unbalancing involves rewarding the hardworking individual with the time to play hard. Some fun! Not too long ago, play was proscribed even for children. Harry Emerson Fosdick quotes some of the rules of an American school in 1784: "We prohibit play in the strongest terms. ... the students shall be indulged with nothing the world calls play. Let this rule be observed with strictest nicety, for those who play when they are young will play when they are old." The antidote for this rule may well be the idea of a man I recently heard about, who, in trying to encourage playfulness on college campuses, had the delightful notion to ask for volunteers to walk along some of the buildings on stilts so that they might cheer up fellow students working in second-floor classrooms.

The word "school" comes from the Greek *schole*, which means "leisure." Schools were places in which people could be away from the workaday world so that they had the leisure to play with ideas. Our schools have practically stamped out the playful spirit. Studies are work-oriented and school is to be taken seriously. Class*work* is followed by home*work* and even those who play are really working for rewards. From Little League to big-time collegiate competition, winning, if not the only thing, is practically everything.

Many adults have never known playfulness, even in childhood. They were "born old" and on their own, even from the beginning, like baby snakes. These sober, serious-visaged individuals had times in their lives when they were young, but no real childhoods. They tend to live in an unsatisfying world of overwork, wearily going through the spiritless motions programmed by their inner clockworks, waiting for the mechanisms to wind down and final surcease.

In *Love Against Hate*, Karl and Jeanetta Menninger make this telling point: "In our work with psychiatric patients we are constantly impressed by the fact that they are deficient in the capacity to play or at least that they have never been able to develop balanced recreational techniques." Play has opened up avenues toward normality for the clinically disturbed. And, as has been pointed out many times, if play can help sick people, why not the rest of us, too?

"There seems to be a general idea," the Menningers write, "that recreation is all right if one doesn't take it too seriously. My belief is that much the greater danger lies in not taking it seriously enough. If people do not take it seriously enough, the reason may lie not so much in prejudice as in ignorance. The question just what play does for the individual is not yet fully answered; neither is the question why some people learn to play and some do not. These and many other questions relating to the psychology of play deserve the attention of the best scientific minds."

An inquiry into the nature of play is no frivolous speculation. For centuries, philosophers, poets, doctors, and others have considered play quite seriously. "Man only plays," wrote Friedrich Schiller, "when in the full meaning of the word he is a man, and he is only completely a man when he plays. I promise you that the edifice of esthetic art and the still more difficult art of life will be supported by this principle."

At the present time, there is much evidence to suggest to psychiatrists who have considered the problem that if our society's workload were suddenly halved, the population would be unable to discharge the energy thus freed in an acceptable way. With no talent for play, the expected result would be hostility, aggression, homicide, suicide, mental illness, drug addiction, and alcoholism. This is a serious indictment and underscores a growing problem, for the amount of leisure time increases each year. At the same time, our ability to successfully cope with the rising incidence of increasingly complex situations that come at us almost incessantly, is reaching a saturation point. Meaningful relief will come in playful activity. Those who are unable to play will find themselves in an increasingly precarious predicament.

There are signs that play is slowly becoming respectable. Disco dancing has become a social phenomenon. Millions of people are standing on lines for hours in several of our major cities, eager to enjoy the release found within. Disco records and tapes are big business, and some radio stations are already becoming all-disco-music stations. Roller skating on skates with "quiet wheels" is booming and is already being combined with Disco.

Not too long ago, surfing became a life-style for many. It splashed into our consciousnesses not only as an activity but in the media as well. Movies, music, clothing, televison all picked up the surfing motif. Disco, running, skateboarding, and roller skating seem to be supplanting surfing. A couple of weeks ago, I went to hear a number of people speak in person, one of whom was Dr. George Sheehan, the author of *Running and Being* (Simon and Schuster). A nonrunner, I was nevertheless among those who gave him a standing ovation. Dr. Sheehan made the point that in play you become an artist. His parting words were: "Remember the child you were, be the animal you are, and become the saint you could be."

Many people seem to be seeing the same light. They're saying the same things, each in his or her own way, and with the media proliferation, more and more people are listening. It's going to be all right. We're finally moving in the right direction. In *The Farther Reaches of Human Nature* (Viking Press), Abraham H. Maslow says: "Only recently have we become aware, fully aware, from our studies of healthy people, of the creative process, of play, of aesthetic perception, of the meaning of healthy love, of healthy growing and becoming, of healthy education, that every human being is both poet and engineer, both rational and nonrational, both child and adult, both masculine and feminine, both in the psychic world and in the world of nature. Only slowly have we learned what we lose by trying daily to be *only* and *purely* rational, *only* 'scientific,' *only* logical, *only* sensible, *only* practical, *only* responsible."

Dr. George Sheehan: "Play is where life lives. Where the game is the game. At the borders we slip into heresy. Become serious. Lose our sense of humor. Fail to see the incongruities of everything we hold to be important. Right and wrong become problematical. Money, power, position become ends. The game becomes winning. And we lose the good life and the good things that play provides."

Instead of trying to run up the score against an opposing team, it might be more constructive to conduct the play so that the scores are kept close. This might be done by shifting the high scorers or most effective defensive players on teams in the lead to the opposing side. It might be done, as in the Public Broadcasting System's gameshow "We Interrupt This Week," by having the host or moderator arbitrarily assign points for correct answers so that the scores are equalized. If more than lip service is to be given to the proposition that "it's not whether you win or lose but how you play the game," surely these approaches should be considered.

Perhaps the Olympic Games, which have become as intensely competitive as any other big-time sports competition, should consider changing some of the rules so that the aspects of competition among and between nations is deemphasized, as well as some of the competitive aspects between and among individual athletes, as was the original concept. In addition to drug-taking and other forms of outright cheating to gain competitive advantages, there is a vast disparity in the amount of professionalism, government support, and even the size of national populations from among which to choose competitive athletes. Perhaps if teams were put together by the luck of the draw or in some other nonnational fashion, the emphasis would be placed more on the brotherhood of humankind than on winning at any price.

Playfulness is important and we are depriving a large segment of the population of its benefits by our emphasis on winning and losing, which is antithetical to the spirit of playfulness. Erik Erikson, in a thirty-year follow-up of people who had been studied as children, found those "who had the most interesting and fulfilling lives were ones who had managed to keep a sense of playfulness at the center of things." Other researchers have shown that the opportunity for play affects a child's later creativity.

Robert Louis Stevenson wrote in *Child's Play*: "Nothing can stagger a child's faith; he accepts the clumsiest substitutes and can swallow the most staring incongruities. The chair he has just been besieging as a castle, or valiantly cutting to the ground as a dragon, is taken away for the accommodation of a morning visitor, and he is nothing abashed; he can skirmish by the hour with a stationery coal-scuttle; in the midst of the enchanted pleasance, he can see, without sensible shock, the gardener soberly digging potatoes for the day's dinner. He can make abstractions of whatever does not fit into his fable, and he puts his eyes into his pocket, just as we hold our nose in an unsavoury lane. And so it is, that although the ways of children cross with those of their elders in a hundred places daily, they never go in the same direction nor so much as lie in the same elements. So may the telegraph wires intersect the line of the highroad, or so might a landscape painter and a bagman visit the same country, and yet move in different worlds."

Our daughter brought the two kittens which were sharing her dormitory room home for the Thanksgiving weekend. Watching them at play, I was struck by their spontaneity, the way they manipulated the environment, making use of what they could find, incorporating it at once into their enjoyment of the moment. Too many adults take play much too seriously, arguing over the rules of the game, looking to the "directions" for guidance, or invoking Hoyle or some other authority.

There are, however, some hopeful signs. Two out of every five pairs of shoes sold in this country today are some kind of running shoes, and at least some of these runners are doing it because it feels good, simply for the fun of it. The popularity of "The Gong Show" is, I think, an indication that millions of people are willing to watch some highly unprofessional entertainment for the fun of it. A few years ago, when the mood of the country was much more uptight than it is today, I don't think the show would have had a chance. An amateur hour featuring the best available amateur talent might have made it, but bad amateurs surely would have bombed.

The landscape is changing. Not long ago there was an inauguration of the new president of Mount Holyoke College. These ceremonies used to be solemn occasions, but this one was different. The new president, a woman (a first), rode onto the grounds on a horse and pulled a prop sword out of a papier mâché rock, and before you could say "Excalibur," she was installed. Students, some of whom were dressed in appropriate old English garb, cheered. Many floats and more than a half-dozen "knights" on horseback (with our daughter, Leslie, and the riding master in the lead) preceeded the president.

Once playfulness takes root, can Disneylands for adults be far behind? Adult games, electronic and otherwise, are doing well, but somebody will invent a new game in which nobody can lose, like frisbee, and it will sweep the country. The object of the game will be to keep the game going, and players will be able to enter and leave at will.

The interplay with nature will recieve greater attention as an element of playfulness. Children and artists seem to appreciate sunsets and seascapes, snowfalls, and the out-of-doors as part of their territory. Part of the durable charm of the "Singin' in the Rain" sequence from the film of the same name is Gene Kelly's childlike playfulness with the rain, the puddles of water, and the delightfully inventive way the entire setting was utilized to further the enjoyment of the piece, a rare and lovely conception for an adult.

Johan Huizinga, near the end of the first Beacon Paperback edition of his *Homo Ludens* ("Man the Player"), tells us: "So that by a devious route we have reached the following conclusion: real civilization cannot exist in the absence of a certain play element...." He goes on to quote Plato: "'Life must be lived as play, playing certain games, making sacrifices, singing and dancing...'." Robert Louis Stevenson's gentle plea in favor of a child's play doesn't go far enough: "They will come out of their gardens soon enough," he wrote, "and have to go into offices and the witness-box. Spare them yet awhile, O conscientious parent! Let them doze among their playthings yet a little! for who knows what a rough, wayfaring existence lies before them in the future?"

To these words, I would add a few written by George Santayana: "There is an undeniable propriety in calling all the liberal and imaginative activities of man play because they are spontaneous and not carried on under pressure of external necessity or danger.... By play we are designating no longer what is done frivolously but whatever is done spontaneously and for its own sake, whether it have or not an ulterior utility. Play in this sense may be our most useful occupation. So far would a gradual adaptation to the environment be from making play obsolete, that it would tend to abolish work and to make play universal."

And feel that I am
happier than I know.

John Milton
Paradise Lost

Feeling Great

Most people secretly love magic. Not stage magic but the
beguiling alchemy of turning base metals to gold or the secret
of eternal life, of health, wealth, and happiness. These
high-romance attractions are so laden with appeal we want to
believe they're out there for us, maybe around the next corner
or over the next rainbow.

The good news is that we've been right all along. The
magic we've yearned for is on the horizon, clearly sighted.
Medicine, light-years behind the physical sciences for decades,
has finally put on seven-league boots and is taking giant
forward leaps.

I have a strong hunch about the millennium. A startling
number of scientific breakthroughs occurred during the decade
that centered on 1900. There were Madame Curie's experiments with radium, Roentgen's discovery of X rays, Freud's
theories of psychoanalysis, Edison's invention of the movie
projector, the picking up of Marconi's radio signals at a
distance of more than a mile, the automobile, the Wright

brothers' first flight in a heavier-than-air craft, and Einstein's theories, which led to the splitting of the atom, to name only a few that come readily to mind.

As we approach the end, not only of the twentieth century after Christ, but also the end of a millennium, I believe the twenty years that center on the year A.D. 2000 will produce near miracles. This belief, shared by many others, is grounded on the enormous energy and talent and other resources at work on a number of basic problems. In October, 1978, McGraw-Hill issued its *Survey of Technological Breakthroughs*. In the fields of medicine, biology, and chemistry, the following are expected between 1990 and 2010: life expectancy of one hundred years, permanently raised intelligence, a retarding of the aging process, the cure for cancer, a substitute for blood, sight for the now hopelessly blind.

It is a cruel paradox that as these wonderful dreams take on the dimensions of reality, at the very threshold of a bright, new era, when there is so much to live for, so many are choosing to die. The pressures of our life-style have become so disorienting and destructive, suicide is now the third leading cause of death (after accidents and homicides) in the age group fifteen to twenty-four in the United States. Alcoholism and drug addiction afflict additional millions, and those closest to them, not to mention the productivity losses, the crimes that stem from these kindred maladies, and the fatal automobile accidents.

Perhaps less obvious than the effects of stress, but equally life-defeating, are the effects of inadequate exercise, improper diet, and unenlightened attitudes toward our own well-being There is a mountain of evidence that suggests these effects, singly or in combination, shorten tens of millions of lives and needlessly limit and diminish the lives of a like number, to the point that the line between these two groups blurs and they tend to merge. Fortunately, there is a clear path available that leads to a rich, abundant life of vitality, harmony and wholeness, and it beckons.

"Stress," according to Dr. Hans Selye, in the preface of his book *The Stress of Life* (McGraw-Hill), "is essentially the rate of all the wear and tear caused by life." Dr. Selye has been a pioneer in the field of stress and is almost undoubtedly the world's foremost authority on the subject. His thesis is simple. "The secret of health and happiness lies in successful adjustment to the ever-changing conditions on the globe; the penalties for failure in this great process of adaption are disease and unhappiness."

In our daily lives, we cannot avoid stress. Indeed, the total absence of stress would not be desirable. We can, however, learn to minimize the damaging effects of stress, to harmlessly drain off and discharge the thousand "natural shocks the flesh is heir to."

Any physiological or psychological overload can cause stress, as can such specifics as poor diet, overwork, drugs, infections, wounds, noise, diseases, illnesses, lack of sleep, irritation, excitement, pain, pressure, shock. Even a job promotion or a vacation can cause stress. Whatever the causes, the effects can be, and often are, damaging, even fatal. In a dynamic, fast-moving society such as ours, we are continually adapting to, and trying to cope with, countless "future shocks" and almost constant pressure. The accumulated wear and tear on our minds and bodies is alarming. Hypertension, heart attacks, atherosclerosis, brain hemorrhage, kidney disease, and strokes are some of the more obvious effects.

Fortunately, there are a number of simple methods and techniques for reducing your stress levels to manageable proportions. In the late sixties, I became interested in transcendental meditation and in the man who, more than any other person, brought it to the attention of the world, Maharishi Mahesh Yogi. I spoke with Maharishi when he was in Malmö, Sweden, and subsequently met with one of his three "world governors."

Transcendental meditation, or TM, is a method of providing mental and physical relaxation and a cornucopia of benefits that flow from the relaxed state it produces. The metabolic rate is reduced more with TM in a few minutes than it is during an entire night's sleep. By reducing stress, lowering blood pressure, relieving anxiety and tension in a natural way, without the side effects of drugs, TM offers a simple, effective means of restoring the body and eliminating much destructive wear and tear. In short, TM can provide the antidote to the fast pace and high pressure of modern living. By producing "serenity without drugs" (the subtitle of Maharishi's book *Transcendental Meditation*) and getting the nervous system to function efficiently, the package of benefits TM provides includes, according to a large and growing body of scientific experimentation, increased energy and a higher level of intelligence, a better memory, greater productivity, better personal relationships, and a heightened feeling of well-being.

The practice of TM requires about fifteen to twenty minutes twice daily and some personal instructions to ensure that the method has been learned and to supply your own personal mantra. Because of these requirements, it would not be constructive for me to set forth some mantras and general instructions. There would be no way to be certain this course would be helpful and not counterproductive. Those interested in TM may contact a conveniently located TM center near them. In this country alone, there are such centers in every metropolitan area and in every major city.

There are other effective meditation techniques. However, before spelling out any details, I would make the general disclaimer that this book is going to be read by people unknown to me, for some of whom meditation might be unsuitable. Prudence dictates that your own physician or adviser be consulted before you engage in any of the activities that might be suggested by this, or any other, chapter.

Dr. Herbert Benson, author of *The Relaxation Response* (William Morrow), has done considerable research in this field, some of which enlisted the cooperation of Maharishi. Dr. Benson developed a technique of counteracting stresses and their damaging effects. Called the relaxation response, it combines four elements: a quiet environment; a kind of mantra, that is, a simple word or sound which is repeated aloud or mentally; a passive attitude in which you do not worry about how well you are doing in achieving the relaxation response; and a comfortable sitting position.

Precisely how to go about eliciting for yourself the relaxation response is set forth clearly in about a page of Dr. Benson's book. The experimental results of this technique appear to be comparable to those obtained from TM. Those who are interested should be able to find his book in libraries or bookstores.

José Silva, who was mentioned in a previous chapter, has developed a technique he calls "controlled relaxation." This aspect is only a tiny part of Silva Mind Control, but it may serve to introduce some readers to Silva Mind Control. Coincidentally, on the same day I began to write these words, the New York Yankees won the 1978 World Series and Bucky Dent was voted the Most Valuable Player. Both Dent and his former roommate, Rich (Goose) Gossage, both of whom live in the same town in New Jersey, I had been told before the Series began, are Silva Mind Control graduates. If the Silva method had anything to do with the way they performed in the Series, it would seem to have something going for it.

I feel privileged to describe the Silva method of relaxation as I learned it directly from a Silva instructor. The basic technique could not be much simpler. You sit in a comfortable, relaxed position. You take a deep breath and, on exhaling, you mentally repeat and visualize the number three, three times. You take another deep breath and mentally repeat and visualize the number two, three times on exhaling. Another deep breath and mentally repeat and visualize the number one, three times on exhaling. This will produce what Silva calls the basic plane level." You can increase the relaxing effects by counting down from a higher number. These exercises produce a calming, relaxed state of mind and body.

TM, the relaxation response, and controlled relaxation are all effective in reducing the harmful effects of stress. Silva's methods, however, offer many other benefits. His system is taught in a four-day program which gives graduates the right to repeat any or all of the days an unlimited number of times. Those interested may care to read *The Silva Mind Control Method* (Simon and Schuster) by José Silva and Philip Miele or the presentation of the Basic Lecture Series by Silva Mind Control International, Inc., 1110 Cedar, P.O. Box 1149, Laredo, Texas 78040. Jess Stearn's *The Power of Alpha Thinking* (William Morrow) is a fascinating account of the author's actual participation in a course given by an instructor who had studied with José Silva.

Despite the recent popularity of running, jogging, and tennis, most Americans are in poor physical condition. The Kraus-Weber tests have produced consistently disappointing results for Americans. These are six well-researched tests of physical fitness (that measure strength in relation to body weight and flexibility in relation to height) which have been given for years to children in primary and secondary schools and to adults in this country and in several European countries. When it is realized that this test is designed to measure minimal physical fitness, the failure rate among Americans is abysmal.

Most of those who do any physical exercise, do it too little and too irregularly to condition themselves. Some weekend athletes overdo it and hurt themselves. Tiger Balm, available in some so-called health food stores, may provide relief for many simple muscular aches and pains. In addition to its effectiveness, there are the outlines of a tiger extruded from the side and bottom of the glass jar, which children of all ages should find charming. A nation of out of shape "bad back" sufferers has recently discovered running. Many are punishing themselves by pounding out the miles on hard pavement and in the wrong shoes.

There is a better way to physical fitness. The best approach I've seen is that of Dr. Leonard E. Morehouse. Dr. Morehouse is a Ph.D., a professor of exercise physiology and founding director of the Human Performance Laboratory at UCLA. His credentials are extremely impressive. He is a physician, a former college track man and captain of the UCLA track team, author of the material on physical conditioning and exercise in *The Encyclopaedia Britannica* and *The Encyclopedia Americana.* He is the inventor of an exercise machine and the designer of a program for its use by our Skylab astronauts, both of which were remarkably effective, and he has spent more than forty years in the field of physical fitness. If anybody qualifies as a world authority in his chosen profession, surely it is he. Dr. Morehouse and Leonard Gross have written a valuable book, *Total Fitness in 30 Minutes a Week* (Simon and Schuster).

Dr. Morehouse's fitness program is directed not at athletes or the ill or injured, but at practically everybody else. It is designed to produce certain effects on your heart which are measured by taking your pulse. His method is thus based not on a measurement of your performance of a given regimen of exercise (which may vary considerably), but on a monitoring of your own pulse rate as a measurement of the conditioning effect you are receiving. The amount of weight you lift or the number of times you lift it do not measure how your body is responding to the load. Neither does the speed at which you run, swim, or bicycle nor the distance you cover in so doing.

It is your pulse rate that provides a measurement of the effects of exercise on your body. This is the key difference between Dr. Morehouse's approach and most other methods of fitness training. Fitness is achieved by putting out a certain load of exertion during a prescribed interval, not by being able to perform physical tasks or by beating somebody else in competition. The goal of Dr. Morehouse's program is "better hearts, lungs and blood vessels, firmer bones, stronger muscles." Not a bad package by any means!

The goal is achieved through a program of exercises designed to increase your suppleness, strength, and endurance until you are fit. You are then rather easily maintained at this level. For the specifics, I recommend reading the book by Dr.

Morehouse and Mr. Gross. One caveat we've all heard before: Before attempting any exercise program there are certain minimum criteria of fitness that must be met in order to prevent ill effects, injury, or even death, and Dr. Morehouse offers some good advice and counsel here, too.

Diet is another basic element in any quest for a long, healthy life. This is not the place to recommend specific foods or attempt to plan menus. If you do not have a fairly adequate handle on these areas, there is a mass of easily obtained material on this aspect of the subject in any general library. A good book on the subject is H. L. Newbold's *Mega-Nutrients for Your Nerves* (Peter H. Wyden). Dr. Newbold is an orthomolecular psychiatrist and a respected professional in this field. We have been told for decades that we are a well-nourished nation. While most of us, but by no means all, have a fairly abundant caloric intake, the adequacy (not to say excellence) of our diets, as a nation, is highly exaggerated.

Millions of older people are malnourished. Many live alone and lack the motivation to prepare balanced meals for only one. Others are indigent or ignorant. In fact, to cite the shocking medical opinions of Dr. Emanuel Cheraskin and Dr. W.M. Ringsdorf, Jr., up to 80 percent of the people in this country may be malnourished. Data from the University of Alabama Medical Center indict poor diet as a cause of a host of afflictions from insomnia to cancer. Thus, the American diet may not be well balanced or nutritionally adequate. Processing, hormones, preservatives, shipping, exposure to air, additives, chemicals, and cooking all impair nutritional values and junk foods and nonfoods, stimulants, drugs, tobacco, alcohol, and harsh environmental elements further attenuate the food values of what we eat.

As one's biochemistry is so highly personal, there can really be no intelligent approach to an optimum diet for this or that individual without his or her first having a thorough blood work-up and other testing, including a battery of sublingual (under the tongue) food allergy tests, a five- or six-hour glucose tolerance test, and a T-3 and T-4 thyroid test, competently taken and properly analyzed. Orthomolecular doctors often include a test of the mineral content of your body that involves sending a tablespoon of your hair to a laboratory in Utah. My copper levels were found to be excessive, a common problem, probably caused by drinking lots of tap water drawn through old plumbing.

If you can afford these tests, and they are costly, you should consider them seriously as they provide a baseline from which to move. Not to be aware of these fundamental indicators is analogous to taking a long automobile or airplane trip without instrumentation or gauges or maps. You might arrive at your destination, but the trip may not be pleasant or relaxing and the risks may be foolhardy.

If you do decide with your doctor to have the tests you will, presumably, be able to move toward the norm, based on the results. Specific supplementation of those substances which were found to be deficient and a reduction of intake of those substances for which your levels were above normal should nudge you toward a more desirable balance.

Mineral supplements, in the opinion of several doctors, are ill-advised unless specifically prescribed by a competent doctor. Overdoses of minerals are not harmlessly excreted, and their levels can be raised in your body to your detriment. The hair test referred to will also indicate possible harmful levels of some of the heavy metals, such as mercury and lead. Chelating agents can reduce toxic or dangerous levels.

If you are found to be hypoglycemic or allergic to certain foods, both conditions being extremely common, you will be in a position to make the appropriate adjustments in your diet so that painful and depressing symptoms of these conditions are eliminated. These symptoms are insidious, and their cause is often unsuspected. All too often, foods that are most commonly eaten by an individual, especially in large quantities, are the very ones to which he or she is allergic.

Once your blood chemistry is in good balance, the key to good nutrition lies in eating a variety of intelligently prepared, nutritious food, without overeating, and in omitting or sharply limiting your intake of empty calories, junk food and nonfood. The latter categories would include harmful dyes, table sugar, chemical additives, highly processed foods, artificial colorings, preservatives, hormones, antibiotics, soft drinks, coffee, tea (not including herb teas), tobacco, alcohol, and self-prescribed drugs.

In addition, it would be prudent to make an effort to avoid a long and growing list of known and suspected carcinogens. Over the past ten years, a number of cancer-causing substances have been identified in our food, air, and water. These include vinyl chloride, saccharin, tris (a flame retardant used in children's clothing), asbestos, food preservatives and additives that flavor and color many processed meats, and others, the latest of which to appear in the headlines being nitrite.

The proliferation of these dangerous or potentially dangerous substances in our environment has confused and irritated many people. A number of people are skeptical because many of the tests were conducted on rats and mice or other laboratory animals and involved relatively high intakes. Some have openly questioned the validity of such testing for humans. Others have adopted the attitude that, as so many carcinogenic agents are present, it would be useless to try to avoid all of them.

My view is that it would be foolish not to be aware of the dangers and to take available opportunities to improve the odds in your own favor. We can give ourselves many, many years of lead time by having access to early reports. It often takes ten to twenty-five years before early findings appear in newspaper headlines. One or two subscriptions to even the popular health publications can provide this important margin at moderate cost.

Reports linking asbestos dust to cancer have been extant for more than forty years, for example, but have only recently made the headlines and are currently the subject of litigation. Many scientists think that between 60 and 90 percent of all cancers are caused by environmental factors, including cigarettes and diet. Many of these harmful substances are known, and others will doubtless be discovered. To ignore this evidence is to move away from life. The choice becomes clearer all the time.

What is especially foreboding is the likelihood, still little explored and publicized, that exposure to combinations of carcinogens multiplies the odds against one exponentially. Thus, ignoring the available evidence or allowing yourself to remain unaware of it, is likely to be a costly decision. The intelligence that would suggest the installation of a reliable heat and smoke detector in your home, in order to provide vital lead time and avert a catastrophe in the event of fire, would also suggest acquiring early warnings of other threats to your life and well-being.

A doctor who doesn't consider good nutrition and physical fitness a faddist or foolish pursuit should be able to recommend a couple of publications to which you may subscribe that will be helpful in this context. Much of the responsibility for feeling good lies with each of us. Each one of us may choose at fifty, for example, to have the heart and lungs, blood vessels and blood chemistry, organs and skin of the average thirty-five-year-old or, at the other extreme, the average sixty-five-year-old, assuming we survive to that age at all.

If you are interested in pursuing the nutritional aspects of your health and well-being but are not familiar with doctors who can help you or refer you, you might consider the following two possibilities. The names and addresses of members of the Academy of Orthomolecular Psychiatry nearest you may be gotten from the North Nassau Mental Health Center, 1691 Northern Boulevard, Manhasset, New York 11030, or you may obtain similar information about members of the International College of Applied Nutrition by contacting this organization at P.O. Box 386, La Habra, California 90631.

The importance of full-spectrum light was explained to me by Dr. H. L. Newbold. Dr. John Ott, who as a teen-ager did pioneering work in time-lapse photography, has conducted a number of fascinating experiments at the Environmental Health and Light Research Institute at Sarasota, Florida. Full-spectrum light, the light that comes from the sun, for example, is necessary for maintaining people (and almost undoubtedly, plants and animals as well) in optimum health. Light sources that eliminate parts of the full spectrum are destructive and dangerous. Practically all interior lighting is less than full spectrum (although Dr. Ott has developed a full-spectrum flourescent tube, the Vita-Lite, available from the Duro-Test Corp., 1710 Willow St., Fairlawn, New Jersey).

Emotional health, metabolic control, calcium absorption, even sexual function, are all improved by exposure to full-spectrum light, and its absence is linked to depression, irritability, instability, poor interpersonal relationships, lowered productivity, and a marked increase in antisocial behavior. Evidence based on experiments with laboratory animals consistently indicates that those raised in full-spectrum light, real or artificial, have larger sexual glands and smaller spleens than those raised under standard artificial lighting.

Interestingly, almost all window glass and eyeglass lenses block full-spectrum light and are therefore detrimental. However, available in the marketplace are lenses (for both spectacles and contacts) as well as window glass, made of a plastic that admits full-spectrum light. These products and the Vita-Lite should be considered by people confined to the indoors or who exhibit any of the symptoms associated with the deprivation of full-spectrum light, including hyperactivity in children. Others might profit by increased exposure to outdoor daylight (without wearing glasses and contact lenses that admit less than full-spectrum light). Direct exposure to sunlight is not necessary, as full-spectrum light is also available in the outdoor shade, so those sensitive to such direct exposure need not deprive themselves for this reason.

A suitable music bath may provide a desirable and salubrious treatment. You may record your own selections on blank audio cassettes so that, depending upon your moods and desire, you may select tranquilizing, calming sounds or stimulating music. Recorded sound effects are also available. Crashing surf, pounding rain, and bird calls may be helpful in producing a relaxing of tension and may also promote restful sleep. Recorded "white" noise can make the sleep-disturbing sounds of motorcycles, buses, and trucks and the clink-clang of loose manhole covers tolerable. Drapes and carpeting, tightened floorboards, pitch darkness, and the elimination of loud-ticking clocks and dripping faucets also help to ensure a continuous night's sleep.

For relief of the pain of eyestrain, you might consider a towel wrung out in extremely hot water, rolled up and placed over the eyes while you lie in a supine position. If this is not convenient, you might try rubbing your palms together vigorously until the friction produces a good heat. Then, cup your hands over your eyes with the fingers pointing up toward your hairline. The heat and darkness provide a wonderfully relaxing, calming effect.

There is a growing body of evidence that suggests our attitudes are of crucial importance to our well-being. Physical illness may, in fact, reflect a kind of "sickness of the soul," a spiritual dis-ease. Western medicine is at last opening itself to the possibility that cures and therapies outside of its traditional approaches are effective and should no longer be ridiculed or ignored.

In 1901, Webster's Unabridged Dictionary defined "uranium" as a "worthless white metal not found in the United States." Tell that to the people at Westinghouse Electric, who recently heard a court decision that may ultimately cost hundreds of millions of dollars on contracts to supply that "worthless" mineral. Uranium didn't change its properties. It was always of potential value. What changed was our understanding and appreciation of its potential. The same kinds of fundamental changes of attitude are taking place with respect to our concept of healing, of health and well-being.

There is a shift toward treating the individual as a whole

instead of as a collection of parts. This holistic approach emphasizes the inseparability of mind and body in the treatment of disease and the importance not only of treating and preventing disease but also producing wellness, as well as the role of the individual as a self-healer. "The most important thing to know about healing," says Dr. Irving Oyle in *The Healing Mind* (published by Celestial Arts and reprinted by Pocket Books), "is that nobody does it. You either heal yourself by stopping all ego-centered activity or you actively impede the process." There is certainly room for both holistic and traditonal Western as well as other modes of treatment, prevention, cure of illness, and the production of wellness.

At the turn of the present century, the leading causes of death in this country were directly or indirectly related to infections. Today, deaths due to infections are almost one-sixth as common as they were in 1901. The chronic diseases are the medical killers in the United States at the present time: heart disease, cancer, cerebrovascular lesions, arteriosclerosis, and diabetes. There is evidence to suggest, according to Dr. Oyle, that "cancer, arthritis, heart disease, and stroke are likely to be bodily states induced by an unconscious command or picture of self-destruction." Dr. Oyle believes that the part of the brain that has learned to produce many illnesses in our bodies as a result of an "inappropriate" response to stress can be retrained through biofeedback, which would permit us to understand the effects on our bodies and allow us to make the necessary corrections.

It may be much more appropriate to ask yourself the reason you are ill than to reach for the nearest handy drug. On the rare occasions when I am feeling ill, I have learned to ask myself why and to look for what may have gone wrong in my life as a cause of the illness. I have made the discovery through this simple process that a thickening packet of unpaid bills at times when my funds were low often triggered a physical reaction, particularly if expected and awaited income failed to materialize as promised. After years of suffering a series of throat infections induced by postnasal drip from an infected sinus, I am now able to eliminate this cause of illness. I can look at a thick packet of bills and see only bills and not a threat to my well-being or self-esteem. The bills will all be paid in full, and there is no longer any need for me to become ill about them.

For another personal example, I recently awoke with an extremely painful stiff neck. In asking myself why, it suddenly occurred to me that the previous day I had learned that a man intended to withhold payment to me of about twenty thousand dollars. I had permitted this man to literally give me a pain in the neck. These personal examples are typical of the psychogenic causes of many common ills, and an understanding of the linkage that triggers them may help prevent them.

The mental component of health can hardly be overestimated, although it seems to have been long underestimated when not entirely ignored. The attempt to split and isolate into separate compartments everything under the sun has led nowhere. Slowly, but inexorably, the concept is being accepted that everything is interrelated. Perhaps the common denominator is consciousness or energy or vibrations or something even more elementary. Whatever it may be, it is becoming apparent that to be in good health requires a harmonious total environment, a properly aligned relationship of the part we call "self" to all that we may now look upon as "other than self." Perhaps the day is not too far distant when the connection between "self" and "other than self" is clearly recognized.

If anybody told me being a newsboy
builds character, I'd know he was a liar.

Young newspaper deliverer
quoted in *Working*
by Studs Terkel

Working

The current concept of work is remarkably different from what it was when our grandparents were our age. Two generations ago there were few women in the so-called labor force. Young men and boys began to work at an early age and were employed, usually in the same kind of work, for the rest of their lives. Early retirement or, for that matter, retirement of any kind, was rare. Men worked until they were unable to do so, and they died on the job or shortly after their enforced retirement. Those who succeeded did so gradually, over a long period of time. Under the tutelage of older and more experienced supervisors, one began to "climb the rungs" of the enterprise. It was a long-term process, and one had "a life's work." There was also a tendency to follow in one's father's (or at least older brother's) footsteps. There was a tradition of the family business, craft, or profession. "And sons," was a not uncommon addition to the names of companies, and it was a proud day for the entire family when this change was made official.

Most of the population lived in rural areas. Farming, mostly a small, family enterprise, was the occupation of a relatively large percentage of Americans. The farm workday began before sunrise and often lasted until bedtime. Those who worked, including children, were expected to do so at least six long days per week, and there were few holidays. Pensions and retirement plans, both public and private, were almost unheard of.

Today, people speak less of "work" than of "a career." The physicality of manual and factory labor have been largely eliminated by machinery and technology. The farm and the factory have been superseded as the nation's workplace by the office. The blue collar has been replaced by the white, and nothing heavier than papers need be handled by most of the nation's employed. The population has moved from small towns to big cities and their surrounding suburbs. Paved roads and automobiles, both ubiquitous, now provide ready, if destructive, access to the cities. Mobility has led to travel and transience.

Our current dynamic, superindustrial, fluid economy presents employment opportunities undreamed of even as few as ten years ago, and the rate of change appears to be increasing. With the employment figures in this country approaching one hundred million in a more than a trillion-and-a-half-dollar economy, a little skill and knowledge and some good planning can provide almost any reasonable career opportunity you may have in mind. Even people who may consider themselves not in the market for a new job or, indeed, for any employment at all, may do well to consider acquiring these tools.

Situations change, sometimes precipitously. Even the most secure positions may be eliminated by virtue of corporate mergers and acquisitions or spinoffs of the part of the company in which you are currently employed. Technological or economic factors may close other companies. You may become seriously ill or incapacitated. Your company may relocate without you. In addition, with the divorce rate soaring, even happily married women who have voluntarily removed themselves from the labor market for years may suddenly find themselves in need of supplemental, not to say sustenance, income. Advance planning does not denote disloyalty to your spouse, and it may even serve to take the pressure off a difficult domestic situation. In fact, with our persistently high inflation rate, more and more women who remain married are entering the ranks of the employed daily, as a means of maintaining a high standard of living.

The nation's concept of work is going to change radically. The number of those not on payrolls is rising at a faster rate than that of the working population. The tax burden on the employed to help support those not working has risen to levels bordering on unacceptable. As health improves and life expectancy increases, and as the growth in the number of the employed slows because of the reduced birth rate, increasing numbers of older, retired people will be returning to the work force.

A friend of mine told me about a man named John Crystal who developed a fascinating approach to helping people discover and/or change careers. For those interested, a twelve-week course is available at the John C. Crystal Center, 894 Plandome Rd., Manhasset, N.Y. 11030. In Crystal's view, personnel departments of large corporations, more often than not, screen out applicants whose backgrounds are not a close match with the available position. Personnel is also often unaware of the most attractive offerings in their own company. In fact, some of the best jobs are those that are created for the particular applicant, and these, by definition, would never find their way into the personnel department.

At the same time, employment agencies and other placement services are biased, as Crystal sees it, in favor of the companies with which they deal on a continuing basis and not the job applicant, who is a one-shot source of revenue. There is a tendency, therefore, to protect the relationship with the corporate client and a concomitant inclination to play it safe by not giving the person seeking the employment opportunity a maximum chance for growth and change. This combines to limit the individual to those situations for which he or she is overqualified and puts a relatively low ceiling on their initial thrust.

Crystal's approach is to seek a better insight and overview of the individual seeking employment in terms of who the person is and what he or she likes to do. He would have you write a long, detailed autobiography, emphasizing your employment background, if any. You would include what you are good at doing as well as what you most enjoy doing, without necessarily attempting to limit yourself to specific career titles. This exercise would create a kind of cross-sectional view of yourself, and from this examination would emerge a new focus that would translate into one or more career directions. An important clue in this connection would be anything you would like to change for the better, however long-range such a project might be. This method, in effect, seeks to tailor a career to your specifications instead of trying to force you to fit an available job slot. The job opportunities that emerge from this process are much more likely to be enjoyable and fulfilling than is usually the case because the focus is on what you want to do at all times.

Once the scanning of yourself has yielded a direction, you begin to hone in on a particular industry or industries that seem to be a good match for you. You would then list, and rank in order of your preference, the specific companies in the field or fields you would most like to join. This presumes some additional homework on your part, which includes learning as much as you can about the specific characteristics of the companies and your chances for advancement in each of them. When this has been completed, the next step is to learn which individuals within each company has the authority to hire you. Some effort and ingenuity are required to accomplish this, but the rewards are more than worth the labors.

The objective is to enable you not only to become employed in the industry of your choice, but by one of the companies with which you would most like to become associated. From a standing start, this approach also gives you about the best possible entry-level position you can handle as well as some personal contact with somebody well placed inside the company who can help you move on from there.

When you have discovered who, in the companies you have selected, are the people in charge of the departments you want to join, you must wrestle with the problem of having a meeting set up with these people. What you want is a personal meeting, not a telephone conversation and not an opportunity to mail in your resume. Nothing but a face-to-face meeting, however short its length, is your objective.

This meeting will give the other person an opportunity to make all of the observations outlined in detail in previous chapters, and you should be prepared to present yourself at your best. If you are not confident you can do this, rehearse with other people of lesser importance to your objective. Any ethical means, direct or indirect, for setting up this meeting should be used. If nobody you know can help you in this regard, there is another way to go.

It is not especially difficult to set up brief, in-person appointments with many well-placed people in the companies on your list, even if they are not in the particular department or area of the company that interests you. If you assure this person (or his or her secretary) you are not asking for a job but wish to get some advice and direction within the industry and explain you are calling this executive because you know he or she is experienced, knowledgeable, and straightforward and will probably be kind enough to see you for ten minutes at his or her convenience, a meeting can usually be arranged. The idea is to obtain the help of this person in setting up a meeting for you within the department or area of your choice.

A number of my friends and business associates have made themselves available to people from within, as well as outside of, their respective corporations. These requests came directly from the particular individual involved or through a mutual acquaintance. Sometimes a good job offer was the direct result. Some executives consider that such requests go with the territory and are surprisingly accessible. This is not to imply that you will be able to see the chief executive officers of major corporations, but you should be able to meet with a number of people in the second and third management tier, and these people can probably do you the most good. You will have varying amounts of empathy with the people you see and, although you should thank and acknowledge each person who is kind enough to see you, try to continue the relationship with those with whom you have some community of feeling.

This technique may also be extremely useful after you are employed by one of the companies of your choice. The following example involves the use of this approach within the company, but it may also be used to meet executives outside the company. A young woman employed by a large corporation called a friend of mine, who was a vice-president in a different division of the company, and asked for a few minutes of his time and some career guidance.

My friend was close to top management, had a great view of the inner workings of the corporation, a keen ear to the ground and was willing to try to be of help. They met briefly at his office. The woman explained her interest in effecting a job change within the company. When asked why she hadn't approached somebody at or near the top of her own department, she explained she wanted to move out of that department but didn't know how to go about it. What she sought was some more general advice from somebody with an overview of the company. She also discussed two or three possibilities which the personnel department had circulated within the company. My friend did not recommend any of these positions, and the woman asked whether he'd mind her calling occasionally to get his advice on other leads. She communicated her resourcefulness and purposefulness and a positive, upbeat frame of mind.

A short time later, she called with a suggestion. Some of

the company's divisions manufactured consumer items. Her idea was the establishment of a company store. It wasn't a "stop the presses" top priority suggestion, but it deserved further consideration, and she was again demonstrating her initiative in a constructive way. With a little fine tuning, my friend forwarded her proposal to the assistant to the president of the corporation, adding the weight of his own good offices to her suggestion.

The company still hasn't acted on her presentation, but she received recognition for it and the extremely important element of increased visibility. The assistant to the president recommended her for a job transfer, and she became an executive, in a job she loves, and at a considerably higher salary. When last seen by my friend, she was at a company function, chatting with the president and his assistant and being introduced to the chairman of the board. Her own initiative and presentation of herself enhanced her visibility and led to a pivotal change for her, with every reason to assume she will go on from there.

Another technique for accelerating job changes and promotions is self-nomination. Instead of waiting for the annual review or whatever method management uses to keep profit margins high without completely destroying employee morale, you ask for a specific promotion to an available job opening or to a slot you create. Your reason for the request should be stated from the point of view of the company. You want to be able to make a greater contribution to the corporation. That's why you seek this new position, not because it fits snugly with your economic needs and/or power drives.

Properly executed, this technique of self-nomination will create, at a minimum, increased visibility and a preferred position. Even if you don't get the promotion at once, you will have, in effect, expressed, in terms the company readily understands, your desire for advancement, your willingness to take on added responsibility, your initiative in instituting the action taken, and your awareness and acceptance of your own greater self-worth. You have thus staked your claim on future advancement and have created an impetus and expectation in the mind of the recipient of your request.

Your request should be directed to a person who can grant it. Precisely which person is a matter of discretion and should be given thought. When I was involved with consumer complaints, I used to make the distinction between complaining and grumbling. The latter involved telling your friends, relatives, neighbors, and/or associates how terrible a place the world had become, generally and specifically, and that it seemed to be getting worse. Complaining, on the other hand, involved telling your story to somebody who could put matters right for you. Was it necessary to contact the chairperson of the board or the president of the company if you had a problem with a defective toaster and you weren't getting satisfaction? Some chose this route with mixed results. It seemed preferable to bring a matter like a defective toaster to the attention of the person in charge of small appliances. This individual had the ability and the authority to handle the problem, and there was room for further appeals to higher levels, if necessary.

A similar approach will work with corporate self-nomination. Unless you have a friendship or excellent working relationship with top management, your request should be made to a lower-ranking executive, and you should seek a face-to-face meeting with the person you intend to ask. If you are encouraged, you may then thank the person in a memo. If not, you are not committed in writing and you may reevaluate your situation and decide to approach a different executive in a position to help you.

Whether you are applying for a job or are already working at one, it is important to understand what the person to whom you report expects of you. As a general rule, your view of your job and your supervisor's view of your job are startlingly different. You may, for example, think the primary functions of your job are to maintain and control inventories and to act as liaison with the factory. To the person to whom you report, the sine qua non of your job is to eliminate headaches for the person to whom you report. Period. If you are successful in that objective, you are assured of his or her support. If you fail your supervisor in this function, you will have an enemy in your camp and your future progress in that department will be blocked as long as this supervisor is in power, no matter how well you may, in fact, be acquitting the particular functions of your job you consider crucial.

The elimination of headaches is such a common requirement among bosses and others in positions to hire and promote you, it may be assumed as a given and used to your own advantage, as in the following example. Mason Adams once found himself among a roomful of other talented people, all of whom were being considered for a voice-over in connection with the production of some television commercials for a new product. The voice of the applicant selected was to be used to help personify the product. Animation techniques would further strengthen the illusion of personality for the product, but the voice had to be right. The applicants were all told that the product was a pencil.

After a number of actors and actresses had read for the part, it was Adams' turn.

"This pencil," he queried, "is it mechanical or wood-clenched?"

The casting director, whose morning had not gone smoothly, put down his Rolaids and looked at Adams for a long moment.

"Wood-clenched," he replied.

"Is it round or hexagonal," asked Adams.

"Hexagonal," said the casting director, the fatigue and the worry no longer visible in his eyes. He had found the person who could eliminate this headache for him.

The man or woman to whom you report has tremendous impact on your life. All too often, you are likely to look upon this person as incompetent, mentally deranged, mean, overly demanding, petty, insecure, unapproachable, short-tempered, dishonest, dictatorial, egocentric, inconsiderate, volatile, sadistic, and miserly, or as possessing some combination of these qualities. This somewhat biased point of view creates a formidable, even insurmountable, barrier to a good working relationship and entirely precludes a social relationship. As you saw in another chapter, every bad situation presents a golden opportunity for you to convert it into an unmitigated disaster. The former is simply another problem which can be handled in a number of ways. Catastrophes, however, present little, if any, room in which to maneuver. All but the most committed to self-destruction will prevent such costly conversions.

If your working relationship with the boss is unsatisfactory, it can be improved or finessed, but the emotional charge you are almost undoubtedly putting on the bad relationship is probably adding to its damaging effects on you. It is important to reduce the scale of the problem by first confining its negative consequences. It is certainly within your power to decide not to permit this set of circumstances, no matter how onerous, to carry over into and affect the nonbusiness aspects of your life, your relationships with family and friends, your health, etc.

This decision will immediately limit the damages and remove some of the pressure on you. The relationship may then be considered more objectively. A mutual interest or a mutual friend may enable both of you to bridge the separations between you. Many supervisors and bosses take great interest in somebody who is loyal to them and can provide a strong buffer between themselves and on-the-job problems. By seeking ways to complement the superordinate's weaknesses with your own strengths and initiative, you may be able to induce the porcupine to retract its quills in your presence. With a little luck, particularly if you are thus of help in the boss's advancement, the two of you may even become a team.

Sometimes, however, despite your best efforts, the boss may create what you consider to be an intolerable situation or an invitation to resign. Your annual pay rise may be omitted, or it may be embarrassingly, even insultingly, infinitesimal. Somebody from within the company or from outside of it may be promoted and interposed between the boss and yourself so that you are no longer reporting to your former supervisor but somebody with a lesser job title or of lower status. You may routinely receive only the worst assignments, while your colleagues in equivalent positions share the plums.

The handwriting on the wall is writ large, and the walls themselves seem to be closing in on you. You are deeply offended and hurt by this treatment, and you intend to show this so-and-so that he or she can't do this to you. You may even begin to type your letter of resignation and be planning to fling it onto the boss's desk, or you may be rehearsing your farewell address, in which the boss will finally hear exactly what you think of him or her.

If you are considering this self-destructive pattern of behavior, I respectfully urge you to stop and rethink the position calmly and rationally. If you are reasonably competent at your job, the boss will find it difficult, even impossible in some companies, to fire you unless you do something inordinately stupid or criminal. You have made an investment in this position and to leave it without first securing a better job represents a loss you don't have to take unless you inflict it upon yourself. This is an extremely common mistake and a particularly damaging one. Avoid it.

Should you decide, after due deliberation, to leave your job, it is essential you do so at your own convenience, not that of somebody else. There can be no excuse for voluntarily cutting yourself off from income, benefits, a veritable supermarket of job opportunities within your own company, and the relative ease of going from one job to another as compared with trying the hazards of going from the ranks of the unemployed to a good job, particularly in the face of the less than glowing reference you're likely to get from the boss who so recently received your farewell address.

Are you prepared for this difficult (but necessary) exercise? Get a firm grip on your ego with your right hand and throw it over your left shoulder onto your bed. Let it sit there. It won't get bruised, and it will remain intact and easily retrievable. If you have this important decision to make, it is absolutely essential you do so rationally without guidance from your ego. Look at the realities of the situation. Apart from the shock and the hurt your ego may have sustained, your position isn't really so bad and you can only make it worse by quitting precipitously.

I know many people who faced this problem and can think of only two who hung in and rode it out. In both cases, they actually wound up reporting to a former subordinate. Bottom line: They are currently averaging more than one hundred thousand dollars in annual salaries plus sizable vested retirement benefits, lots of stock in the corporation, and they and their families are almost certainly much better off than they would have been had these executives quit in pique.

Unless your company is about to go into bankruptcy, or is being acquired, or some such unusual exception is present, this is a good time not to act hastily but to learn something about yourself. The chances are excellent that if you are considering quitting your job over an incident along the lines described, the root cause is not incompetence or poor job performance, but bad (or insufficiently good) personal relationships. This unpleasant situation points up the need to become more skillful in your personal relationships, so that your future may at last be free of these unnecessary shocks and crises. Assessments of who is at fault are almost completely irrelevant. Your personal relationships are not likely to improve until you accept full responsibility for them.

Don't permit this event to cloud and color your thinking. You must still feel good about yourself. This experience, if properly handled, will enhance your life, not diminish it; if it doesn't, you are preparing the groundwork for unpleasant repetitions. It is doubly important that you function at your best level. Look good, communicate, relate to others harmoniously, creatively, and without acrimony. Don't suddenly go off on vacation or into hibernation. These actions will only serve to increase the separations between yourself and others.

Unless you have been having conversations with prospective employers and have been seriously considering leaving the position you have, it is almost always a grave error to resign under the circumstances indicated. You are going to need all the help you can get, and your resignation will cut you off from the source of much of this assistance. The mere fact that your expectations have been disappointed need not provoke this sort of overreaction.

Your resignation will make the task of finding another job much more difficult. In most cases, a prospective employee is much more attractive, particularly at a relatively high-level job, if he or she comes from another company and not from the great outdoors, and the deal you can cut will usually be much better in the former cases. If you do resign, you will be under much pressure to provide continuity of income and time will be working against you.

It is important to make time your ally, and this is best done by continuing in your current employment and building your personal network of helpers as set forth in another chapter. These sources will provide the information you need with respect to what openings are, or soon will be, available to you in other companies (as well as your own). The personal helpers you have assembled will also be able, in many instances, to arrange a personal introduction to the individual who can hire you. Information and personal introductions and recommendations are the keys that open important company doors for those who go on to better and better jobs with different business organizations. Without this kind of help or the services of competent professionals, you are alone and at a severe disadvantage. If you haven't spent the time and effort needed to build your own network of helpers, this crisis may provide the impetus to do so.

It will take time for you to develop a good team, of which you will be a proud and contributing (as well as contributed to) member, but time, in this case, will be your friend and ally. When you have thus woven a good safety net for yourself, you may find that the person who engineered this unpleasant incident is working for another company, the one who was brought in to take the job you wanted has been given the former's responsibilities, and you have been promoted into the slot thus vacated. In any event, this experience, if used constructively, will permit you to improve your chances for future success instead of stunting your career and subjecting yourself and those closest to you to unnecessary hardships.

Most large corporations have available to their employees a number of fringe benefits that are not automatically dealt out. They require some initiative on your part if you want to convert them into an asset. For example, the company will usually pay about half at least of the cost of any education you may want to acquire if it is reasonably job-related. While I was working in one department at one of the television networks, for example, I was preparing myself for a promotion into another department. I'd applied for the first job in order to make a transitional move into a field that greatly appealed to me, although the available job would not ordinarily have been my first choice.

While on the job, I took a Master of Fine Arts in film, radio, and television, for which the company paid half the cost and the state paid most of the balance. This broadened my investment in media and the company's investment in me. I took the work seriously, learned much, and did well. The grades became part of my personnel record, as there was some rule about a grade below which the company would not accept any liability for reimbursement.

When the time came to nominate myself for a job change, the man to whom I reported was helpful, for which I was and am most grateful, and the company was happy to have me in a position to make a greater contribution. The company had a stake in my career.

In addition to education, any skills you acquire on the job or on your own may be combined with your other qualifications and transformed into new opportunities for self-nomination. If you have been doing auto body and fender work, this would not ordinarily qualify you for brain surgery, but in less extreme cases there certainly need not be a perfect match between your particular strengths and skills and those you might consider essential for the job. Some people, like great imposters, are able to function in an amazingly wide range of professional and business capacities. They are not inhibited or defensive when applying for such positions (for which, by ordinary standards, they are totally unqualified), and they manage to drift in and out of a variety of vocations with the greatest of ease.

In getting and changing jobs, you will, presumably, be much more responsible than these imposters, but surely you need not dwell on your lack of certain credentials and qualifications often deemed essential, nor should you be defensive about not having them. Many employers are beginning to realize that rigid requirements and overqualifications are not providing optimum results for them. Your emphasis should be on why you think you can handle the job, how well you have performed in the past, your excellent personal relationships and communication skills, and your general enthusiasm.

Should the worst happen and you fail on the job, that is not a catastrophe and, in fact, it may present you with a great opportunity to "fail upward." A number of people have been fired from good jobs, sometimes after only a short time, and have gone out and gotten better jobs. Some Hollywood movie producers bring in picture after picture that bombs at the box office, yet they not only get financing for their subsequent films, the budgets keep going higher and higher. People who fail upward don't take their failures personally. If you should ask them what went wrong, and people rarely do (and the question is even less frequently favored with a meaningful answer), it never seems to have anything to do with them.

Those who make the most productive use of their career time usually have fallback, or contingency, plans so that they never lose their momentum, even if they have a job suddenly shot out from under them. In the past, people were forced to choose a career much too early, long before they were prepared to do so, and they tended to remain in the same general field for a lifetime. There is much more mobility in today's job market. An increasing number of people are having serial careers, that is, making dramatic switches along the way, sometimes pausing to gain work-related experience or additional education in order to facilitate the transition. Young people who had dropped out and older people who had been farmed out while still able to make an important contribution, are coming back into productive work. The experience has been good for the participants and for our society. There is a strong trend in this direction, as increasing numbers of people are learning they need not be tied to a field of interest that previously attracted them or into which they had somehow stumbled but which no longer excites or engages them. Age, sex, race, religion, national origin, background, experience, education, and physical location no longer serve to automatically disqualify or discourage the thousands who are discovering they may enter new fields, make important contributions, and lead more fulfilled lives.

Work is beginning to be more fun and vice versa as the concepts slowly merge. People of college age are visiting the workplaces of successful people in the fields of their choice. The concept of the job is slowly becoming more realistic and less based on the movie or television versions.

In a dynamic environment, the opportunities are manifold. The corporation itself may be viewed as a marketplace in which changes may be created and encouraged. Lunch may be used as an exploratory period in which to broaden the base of your personal relationships with the focus on mobility. With communication and transportation so highly developed, you are not limited to the city or town in which you happen to be living. The entire world is becoming a vast marketplace.

Our emphasis has been on attaining a satisfactory measure of success and building upon it in an efficient way. In so doing, however, it is essential that you give full value in all of your undertakings. You must be willing to put in the hours and to make a contribution no matter what your job, who your supervisor, or what others may be doing. You should be able to grasp quickly the four or five essential elements that probably comprise at least ninety percent of the productivity of the job and place your emphasis on these aspects. Understand clearly how your job relates to your department and how the pieces of the organization fit together, and focus your energy and your will along lines that permit you to make the most meaningful contributions you can. This focused and unstinting approach should assure your success, but don't get carried away with it. Wear your achievements lightly, for at a point success itself may have to be dealt with lest it preempt your continued growth.

> In all negotiations of difficulty,
> a man may not look to sow and reap
> at once, but must prepare business,
> and so ripen it by degrees.
>
> Francis Bacon

Dealing

The media report details of negotiations every day. A big building downtown is bought and sold; the Strategic Arms Limitation Treaty appears headed for agreement; federal mediators meet with both sides in a labor dispute; President Carter, Prime Minister Begin, and President Sadat reach an accord at Camp David. The concept of "negotiating" also applies to transactions that never receive any publicity, dealings that you and I enter into regularly. Many of the same principles that apply to big deals between and among giant corporations and conglomerates, heads of government, and representatives of political, business, labor, and other large interest groups also apply to our everyday lives. You and I may also be or become skilled negotiators.

The *Oxford English Dictionary* lists, as its first definition of the verb "negotiate," "to hold communication or conference for the purpose of arranging some matter by mutual agreement; to discuss a matter with a view to some settlement or compromise." When you buy a new or used car or sell your old one, you negotiate. In renting or buying a place to live or work, you negotiate. In fact, you are likely to be involved in the negotiating process when you get a job or promotion, when you marry, separate, or divorce, when you hire and fire others, when you make a consumer complaint, when you sign a contract. Negotiations may even take place when two couples decide on where to have dinner or which movie to see. In short, we all do a great deal of negotiating, whether we fully realize it or not.

Effective negotiating requires certain skills and attitudes, all of which may be acquired fairly easily. Mastered and practiced, they will serve you well in a multiplicity of everyday transactions. They will enable you to make agreements that please you and make you happy instead of those you are forced, or must learn, to live with.

The first principle in any serious negotiating is to focus your efforts on "the big picture." No matter how complicated the deal, there are almost invariably two or three, perhaps four, elements that, in the aggregate, bulk the lion's share of what we want. The other points, even if there are scores of them, are of little significance to us. This is not to imply that these latter points have no value at all. The other side may place a high value on some of them, and they may be used as trading cards and dealt away in order to nail down one or more of the elements we consider important. The two (or more) sides in negotiations often value some of the various elements quite differently. If you can discern which elements they view as major you are in a better position to trade off what is inessential for you in exchange for a key element.

Next, it is important to understand that you are in a negotiation, not a war. Your objective is to make a good deal, not to destroy the other side. You will fare much better in the long run if you show some give, some willingness to compromise. Unconditional surrender should not be the objective.

This is not to say that you will show weakness in your negotiating stance or that you will continually lead with offers to compromise. In fact, it is important not to do so and it sets a good tone for your side if you are able to extract the first concession or offer to compromise from the other side. But the best deal is one that gives each side something it wants and allows all of the parties to keep their self-respect. In addition, people don't like to be stomped or steamrollered, and they tend to react, sometimes in ways that kill the deal you thought was settled or leave you with a costly, time-consuming lawsuit instead of a good deal.

Sometimes, after you reach a verbal meeting of minds, the other side, in the contract or deal memo that follows will add a sweetener, an additional little something extra for itself that was not part of the agreement, or do a little subtraction from what you were to receive. Or, the other side may attempt to do so verbally, prior to sending written confirmation. This action has to be weighed. If the item they've added for themselves or taken away from me is relatively unimportant, I may allow them to have it.

For example, I was once negotiating a contract for my nonexclusive services and the process was going along extremely well. It was a rather uncomplicated deal. The basic agreement was arrived at quickly, but when the letter agreement arrived, the payment clause called for less than the amount originally agreed. The covering letter explained that although they had agreed to a higher payment, they thought it would create a problem if I got more than everybody else who was similarly contributing to their project, and they promised to make up the difference if their venture proved successful.

Payment for my services was certainly one of the key elements from my point of view, and I could have argued the point and probably won it, but the deal, taken as a whole, was still attractive and the lesser payment was not an unreasonable fee. The job itself was a challenge, and it presented an opportunity to establish my credentials in a new area. I liked the people in charge of the project, and I wanted to establish a good relationship with them. I also wanted to introduce more harmony and wholeness into my life. I was a bit tired of being "the world's most successful complainer," and I longed to hang up my guns at least until absolutely necessary to strap them on again. I accepted their explanation and have never had cause to regret it.

In this example, I handled my own negotiating, which I like to do despite the old admonition (possibly originated by a lawyer's guild) that a lawyer (or anybody else) who represents himself has a fool for a client. Like other old adages (e.g., "Take care of the little things, and the big things will take care of themselves"), this one is not necessarily applicable to all cases. Lawyers' fees, including those of the considerably less than brilliant and the barely competent, have soared beyond unaided visibility. At hourly rates that not too long ago bought tracts of bottomland, the matter at hand would have to be one "of consequence" (to use the late Antoine de Saint Exupery's phrase) for me to hire a lawyer. There is also the possibility that should you hire such a licensed practitioner, you may discover, sometimes well down the lane, that you have a fool for a lawyer.

It would seem that in a relatively small matter, a high-priced lawyer's services would be prohibitively costly and a low-priced lawyer's efforts, when available, often unavailing. It is also not uncommon that the lawyer who is willing to take on medium-sized cases on a basis that will give him or her a share of the venture in lieu of a fee, is not an expert in the field involved nor is he or she an expert negotiator. There is the additional factor of procrastination and the likelihood of less than thorough preparation that often accompanies it from this source, as successive clients who are billed at hourly rates almost invariably get more immediate attention.

My preference is to seek the services of a good lawyer only in sizable deals or in fields with which I am unfamilair and in which I can hire an expert at a fair price in relation to the deal. Otherwise, I like to handle my own dealings. If it later becomes desirable to buffer myself with a third party, I may do so, but this is usually a tactical maneuver in response to the way the other side is handling itself.

One such reason for hiring an attorney would be to create

a negotiating situation in which your representative had only limited authority. He or she would therefore not be able to make any important concessions without your approval but would be able to obtain concessions from the other side. The timing of the negotiation may also be better controlled in this way without your being personally rude or abrasive. Whether or not the representative can reach you for instructions is within your control, and you may thus delay the negotiating process (within limits) if you choose to do so. Often, the two sides value time quite differently, and your understanding of this consideration can make a difference.

A few years ago, I got into a negotiation with a giant real estate company that had bought the apartment building my family was living in and five contiguous buildings. They planned to demolish the six buildings and erect a large complex of high-priced, co-op apartments. During the process of emptying the buildings of tenants prior to demolition, we were approached and asked what it would take to induce us to move out. As I was a principal, I insisted on dealing only with principals. They agreed and then proceeded to renege on three, increasingly bad, deals, using the bad-faith negotiating tactic I call the Alphonse-Gaston technique. It is important to be aware of this approach as it is all too commonplace.

The first principal with whom I spoke, Alphonse, quickly reached an agreement with me. Gaston, the second principal, then informed me that Alphonse had exceeded his authority in making deal number one, and he offered me deal number two, a substantially less attractive prospect. When I accepted deal two, it was withdrawn, and Alphonse offered me deal three and a "take it or leave it" ultimatum. My family expressed their mounting concern and uneasiness at the rising vacancy rate in the building so I accepted deal three, a fairly shabby offer.

When I received a contract that omitted part of what we were to receive under the terms of deal three, we had another family powwow. The offer was rejected, and I told Alphonse to come back to me last, at which time we would renegotiate. As time passed, four of the six buildings were demolished, a fifth was emptied, and our building contained only three tenants, two of whom had signed agreements to leave.

I had been playing certain legal delaying cards sparingly and still had a few more tucked up my sleeve. The other side had about a ten million dollar project on their hands, and they were eager to build as soon as possible. Time was much more important to them than to us. In fact, at the signing of deal number four, an excellent settlement and one that was worth more than the sum of deals one, two, and three combined, the other side was careful not to upset or offend us, lest I raise our demands further.

Time was the key factor in this negotiation. Each day of delay was worth several thousands of dollars to them. They would begin to lose this sum the moment we were the last tenants in the building. By agreeing to my terms for deal number four, these needless losses were averted. All they had to do was to agree to my terms. We had moved into a hotel but had left our furniture in the apartment and picked up our mail regularly. The pressure was squarely on them and no longer on us, and they were even kind enough to pay our hotel bill in full, at my suggestion, as part of our agreement.

If time is important to your side of the deal, you may try to set a deadline after which your offer will be canceled or a penalty imposed for delays created by the other side. At the Camp David summit, President Carter used the former tactic. His suggestion of a self-imposed deadline was accepted by Prime Minister Begin and President Sadat. Once the deadline was in place, the two sides were under mounting pressure to come to an agreement.

The penalty for delays is another useful tool that also has psychological, as well as economic, motivations behind it. When, for example, my former landlord refused the counteroffer after deal number three failed to produce a signed agreement, I told them they would have some additional time in which to reconsider my last offer, during which all of the terms would remain the same except that the price for our moving would rise one thousand dollars per calendar day. This surprised them, as after an offer is rejected, the next offer is expected at a lower, not higher, price. It also made it unmistakably clear that I was aware of the value they placed on time. When they reopened negotiations, I knew they would be happy to go to contract on my terms, without the penalty.

Many people commit the error of making their last offer first. This approach may sometimes be effective if the other side knows from past experience that you will not vary the terms in any particular whatsoever, but even in such cases, you would be presenting an ultimatum, which is not the most acceptable way of negotiating. This may be commendably honorable but there is a bit of self-righteousness behind it which doesn't provide a good environment for bargaining.

A friend of mine was approached by a director of a Fortune 500 company with interest in acquiring his company. After the financial data had been submitted, my friend was asked for his best offer for the company. My friend put his best offer on the table with the declaration that this price was nonnegotiable. When the other side, in disbelief, attempted to negotiate the price, my friend was affronted by their insensitivity to his sense of honor and the negotiations broke down.

A similar result usually is reached when somebody who has suffered some minor but actionable damage attempts to settle with the wrongdoer's insurance company. An inexperienced negotiator, not wishing to spend much time on a small matter, may offer to settle with the most accessible employee of the insurance company and the one with the most limited authority. In such a case, if the last offer is made first, the claims adjustor, all too familiar with inflated claims, will almost invariably reject it. The bottom line is likely to be a failure to reach an agreement with the claims adjustor, and the waste of more time than would have been the case if the damaged party had simply gone through the near-ritual of the negotiating process. The other alternative to not settling at that level of insurance company personnel is a settlement at a lesser figure than was reasonable in order to save time and/or attorney's fees. In these cases it comes down to an understanding of what is customary, which may sometimes resemble the haggling at an Arabian bazaar. Those who do not care to play by the house rules needn't do so, but they should be aware of them.

Sometimes there is a direct route available to those who seek to make a reasonable or honorable settlement quickly but who are being prevented from doing so. Some years ago, some of our property was damaged in moving. The damages were rather small, but the moving company had been paid for packing and unpacking our goods as well as for moving them so that they were clearly responsible but hadn't even called our attention to their negligence.

When what we considered a reasonable claim had been rejected by the movers, instead of bringing a time-consuming legal action or absorbing all or part of the loss, we called the insurance company (whose name was found on the moving contract) that would be reimbursing the moving company. In one telephone conversation with somebody in management, we settled the claim. You can often obtain a better result by getting closer to the person who will ultimately be signing the check.

The other side may occasionally present you with what it characterizes as a "dealblower." This is a term applied to a deal point that will not be yielded even if it means there will be no agreement reached on the entire deal. It is a kind of ultimatum. You must either give up the point or you have no deal. I have been faced with this rather harsh communication and the accompanying implication that if I took too long even considering the withdrawing of the point from the bargaining table, our discussions would terminate.

It is important to remember at such times that an allegation is only an allegation; it need not necessarily be in accord with fact or reality. The other side may subscribe to the poker theory of negotiating and may be bluffing. My personal preference is not to make untrue statements, to avoid bluff and bluster, and to make my own credibility and integrity a valuable tool in the negotiating process, but in some quarters this is still regarded as eccentric.

At any rate, there are many effective responses to ultimatums of this kind. If you are dealing with somebody who is representing a large corporation, the ultimatum may or may not be insisted upon by top management, but this should not be stated or implied early on, as it will only lead to further friction. Don't take unpleasant statements personally, particularly in the context of negotiating. The person you are dealing with is operating out of a set of needs peculiarly his or hers. As your needs are not identical, you don't have to respond in kind. Try to get on with the rest of the deal by suggesting that the other deal points be agreed upon before returning to the sticking points.

However, if the other side insists or if the other points have already been put to bed, I would try to reduce the friction by not responding in the same dogmatic way. If somebody who has the authority to kill a deal you want to make tells you, in effect: "If you don't fold the hand on this point, the deal is off," and you reply: "I refuse and that's final," you are both creating an impasse. Neither wants to lose face by backing down, and both of you can easily keep from losing face by destroying the deal. The demise of the deal becomes an apparently acceptable consequence.

Try to avoid that dead end by patiently but firmly pointing out that what you're asking for seems reasonable and is not at all unusual. In fact, you can express your conviction that the term alleged to be the "deal blower" is becoming so acceptable a standard that you would even agree to substitute a "favored nations" clause in the contract in lieu of the clause itself. The person to whom this is suggested will not want to do this as it would obligate the other side to give you the benefit of any better terms they concede to anybody else. However, it lets the person who gave you the ultimatum know that he or she didn't lay a glove on you with his or her strong statement without being rude and without raising the level of the discord.

At this point, if you've made any concessions in the negotiations, I would point them out to indicate how you had been willing to compromise and suggest that the spirit of compromise should be encouraged by both sides. It is important not to use too many words at this stage or your verbosity will be interpreted as weakness. Be respectful and courteous, but don't be afraid of long pauses. If you have made your points and there is a momentary silence, don't feel impelled to speak. If the other person speaks next, listen carefully in order to catch the nuances, for this is where you may be able to get the subtext of the problem, i.e., what is behind this ultimatum. Is there a company policy or other corporate problem? Does he or she see a problem you don't? Or, is the other side simply bluffing or throwing its weight about in an attempt to bully you?

If the silence becomes unendurable, you may break it with an implied question: "I've been trying to look at this from your point of view, but I can't understand why this gives you a problem." If the other person doesn't respond here in a specific way, or doesn't tell you why he or she won't do so in a convincing way, you're probably being bluffed. It's not really a dealblowing point. There aren't many such points, and they're usually basic and obvious, not recondite. Questions or even implied questions can be helpful in negotiating, but they must be put with skill and used sparingly. In asking, always frame the question in a way that makes it easier to get the answer you want.

If the other person explains his or her reasoning, it will present an opportunity for a compromise. In the last situation of this kind I faced, the reason finally given was that I wasn't entitled to any portion of profits or royalties stemming from the specific contingency I'd raised and that I was being too greedy. I responded by saying that what I was requesting was, in principle, a fairly standard arrangement in the industry, but that I wouldn't insist on 100 percent of the royalties and profits

I was to get under another clause. The other person said he'd take it up with top management.

In the next conversation, he offered 25 percent of the royalties and profits I was to receive under another provision. I first acknowledged and thanked him for discussing the point with management (although I was by no means certain he'd actually done so), but told him I regarded 25 percent as a token payment. I explained it had been my intention to ask for 75 percent and settle for two-thirds. He then offered 50 percent with another ultimatum at high decibel level, and I accepted this offer.

There may be times when the other side deals with you in bad faith, and a deal is unlikely or undesirable. I was once in negotiations with a large corporation, and we had reached agreement on all of the deal points with the exception of a couple of minor items. This had taken approximately three months, mainly because of many unnecessary delays by the other side. My side of the deal was not particularly favorable, and I wasn't particularly pleased with the way the other side had dealt with me. I therefore informed the lawyer with whom I was negotiating that if we were unable to reach an agreement by the close of business that day, I would withdraw from the deal. I think it was clear from my demeanor throughout the prior negotiations that I wasn't bluffing.

With a little effort on their part, we were able to reach an agreement that day, but when the deal memo arrived it was substantially different from our verbal agreement. At that point, I decided there was no further point in pursuing a marginal deal under the circumstances. It was my opinion I was either not being dealt with honorably or the other side was trying to box me into a position from which they could scale down what was already a barely acceptable deal, also objectionable. The written memo so undercut my position that it wasn't worth the effort to try to put the pieces back together, and I had lost the taste for dealing with that company. I therefore broke off negotiations.

Courtesy in negotiating (conspicuously absent in the

above dealing) improves the environment and facilitates the entire process. Avoid making flat, dogmatic statements. Such utterances are abrasive and tend to separate the opposing sides instead of bringing them to a mutual understanding. If you find it necessary to make a pointed remark, don't jab it at the other side with an extra flick or flourish. Try to direct the comment like a shuffleboard puck, allowing it to slide up to its target. A shuffleboard puck, not a pneumatic drill. If you find the deal falling into a favorable groove, give the other side some room in which to maneuver but always be prepared to get something in exchange for every concession you make. Have a mental list of such desirable items ranked in order of their priority for you. Don't give away something for nothing when negotiating. What you should be seeking is a concrete deal-point of value to you and not some vague "goodwill" which you hope later to convert into something of value.

You may occasionally become involved in a tricornered negotiation in which the other two interests are represented by the same person. I was, for example, a plaintiff in actions against two defendants who employed the same law firm to defend them. To encourage them to settle and to upset their coordination, I began to frame my position in ways that surfaced some of the latent conflicts of interest in their positions. Once this was clear, they could not properly be represented by the same lawyers. The increased legal fees that result from hiring two sets of lawyers in such cases have a way of encouraging settlements, particularly when your cause is just.

Sometimes the two sides will vie or feint in an effort to one-up one another. For example, much is sometimes made of the negotiating site. Getting the other side to agree to come to your office is looked upon as a concession, and therefore an advantage, for your side. The other side is thought to be in less control of the variables away from home base, and coming to you suggests deference. While there may be some truth to these assertions, a skilled negotiator can turn a location on the other side's turf to his or her own advantage.

For example, being away may enable the visitor to better control the timing by having to consult with management or the principal if you are negotiating for a third party, or having to consult with an advisor or with reference material not immediately available. Of course, on your own turf you should be a good host or hostess. Provide for the creature comforts of the other side, and be courteous enough to hold the calls and the other details of your everyday schedule.

Experience in negotiating does not necessarily imply expertise, for the experienced negotiator may simply be repeating old mistakes. I once had the misfortune of hiring an attorney to handle a litigation for me who proved to be less than a brilliant negotiator. The matter should never have gone to court, but the other side, clearly and flagrantly in the wrong, steadfastly refused to negotiate or even discuss the matter with me. Reluctantly, I commenced litigation and, with some trepidation, hired a trial lawyer in whom I reposed less than unbridled confidence, despite his tales of large verdicts won and wrongdoers vanquished.

What attracted me to this attorney was his willingness to handle the matter on a straight contingency; that is, his fee would come entirely from the recovery in the matter and there would be no requirement of my putting any money up front. As I considered the case almost impossible to lose and it wasn't a gigantic cause, I preferred not to spend large hourly sums on a matter which, if protracted, might cost me more than I would recover. When the other side refused to negotiate with me, I decided to hire this particular practitioner.

Over the course of more than two years, his creative input was extremely disappointing and his preparation of the case for trial was virtually nonexistent. In addition, despite my repeated requests for him not to do so, this lawyer entreated the other side to settle every time he spoke with them (in my hearing), sometimes even approaching personnel of the defendant corporation who totally lacked the authority to settle for even a quarter. Needless to say, the other side was about as unimpressed with this person's expertise and diligence as I was, and they offered nothing whatever by way of settlement, even when pressed by a judge in pretrial conferences. They continued to offer zero dollars right up to the day I replaced this individual with somebody else.

I cite this example because it is important that clients not be awed by the fact that somebody has been admitted to the practice of law. There are lawyers who handle bushel baskets of matters on a contingent basis, secure in the knowledge that most cases do not go to trial and they will share in the recovery of all of these cases even if they do almost no preparation of the case for trial. However, this lack of preparation will be perceived by able lawyers on the other side, and you may be sure that you as the plaintiff will either get less than you should have by way of settlement or you will have an ill-prepared case should the other side refuse to settle. As time passes, your will and expectations may also be ground down by virtue of this sort of shoddy handling by your lawyer.

If you are not pleased with the handling of negotiations on your behalf, you may always fire your lawyer. The latter may demand a fee for services rendered or, as this attorney did, threaten to sue for *quantum meruit*. As I told this attorney, *quantum meruit* has two aspects: the amount of time spent by the practitioner and the value of that time. In my judgment, the little time spent by this attorney no doubt actually impaired the value of the case. I did pay all of the expenses, secretarial, stenographic, filing fees, disbursements, and a small fee for the attorney, plus thousands of dollars of other costs that were supposed to have been the responsibility of the attorney, and I had no intention of rewarding him further for adversely affecting my interests. He agreed that nothing was owing.

Many lawyers are, of course, competent, and an advantage can be derived from having somebody else aid in negotiating a matter for you. Despite your best intentions, you may not be able to establish a good negotiating environment or a working rapport. Your prior relationship with the other side may have been less than satisfactory, or the personal relationships may break down during the negotiation. A skillful third party, acting on your behalf, may be able to salvage the deal.

You may be faced with a team approach. The other side may designate one member as the "good" person and another as the "bad" one. This overworked device is designed to allow bad news to be imparted to you without impairing your relationship with the "good" person. You should never lose sight of the fact that the team is really a coordinated unit.

Finally, the matter of greed. There are times when one side or the other is so overreaching that the deal finally falls apart. This is particularly unfortunate when a little forebearance would have produced an excellent result for both sides. I heard of a man who was the last holdout on a parcel of land that had been painstakingly assembled over the course of several years in order to construct a big office building in New York City. The man had bought his little building some years earlier for $140,000. The prospective builders had raised their bid for his building from about $300,000 to a rather handsome $1,349,000 before the man agreed to sell.

However, when he arrived to sign the contract, he wanted $1,900,000. Negotiations continued into the small hours of the morning. The bottom line was no deal, and the office building was duly erected around the lone holdout's small building, an unfortunate result and an object lesson to us all in "last straws" and immovable objects.

Making Things Happen

A hundred years ago in this country if you built a better mousetrap, there was a pretty good chance the world would, as the saying has it, "beat a path to your door." Some of those path beaters might try to fleece you out of your better mousetrap, or at least attempt to divert the profits from your pocket to theirs, but your creation had a reasonable chance to reach the marketplace. We don't hear much about paths being beaten to doors of innovators today. Instead, we are told that ideas "are a dime a dozen," and creators and inventors are handed tightly drawn disclosure agreements to sign before major corporations will even look at their intellectual property.

The current reality is that ideas are all too often like trees that fall in forests out of earshot. Ideas are marvelous and necessary, but in order for them to be "produced," they need the contributions of entrepreneurs. These are men and women who organize and manage a business, take the risks, and reap the profits or suffer the losses, the people who take a conception and make it a living reality. They are the ones who make things happen. The big rewards, rightly or wrongly, go not to creators but to entrepreneurs.

A good idea of the weights assigned to entrepreneurs and creators is furnished by the television industry. Next time you watch an episode of a television series (particularly one supplied by an independent company), look closely at the credits. The series may have been created by Tom, produced by Dick, and supplied by Harry's company. The original concept for the series may or may not have been Tom's. It may have originated with Dick or with Harry or one of Harry's employees or somebody else. It may be based upon a play or book or story or movie written by somebody else, and it may have been somebody other than Tom who thought of making it the basis of a television series.

Let us assume, however, for the sake of giving Tom maximum creative input, that it was he who conceived of the original idea for the series; he wrote the pilot without the help of any other writer; he created all of the characters, the situation; and all of the dialogue in the pilot was his. These assumptions are unrealistic, as creative suggestions from suppliers, producers, directors, actors, other writers, and from the network are inevitable.

Everybody whose name you see on the screen gets paid, and their salaries, when they work, are relatively high. The creator of the series, Tom, may have gotten some money for the rights to the basic property, a fee for writing the pilot script (and for any episodes he subsequently writes), plus a per episode royalty for each new episode telecast (with residuals for replays that are scaled down and end after a specified number of replays), and a small percentage of the net profits. In order to have any net profits, a carload of distribution and production expenses will come off the gross of a successful series.

However, Harry, the entrepreneur whose company is supplying the series, will fare handsomely with a successful series. In fact, when you realize that a successful series can gross in the neighborhood of one hundred million dollars, compared with the entrepreneurs who supply these episodes, everybody else, with all due respect to some extremely creative and talented individuals, is just labor.

Certainly not all entrepreneurs are successful and not everybody wants to be an entrepreneur. Indeed, entrepreneurs are often overworked, neglect their families, and have little time for friends, and the failure rate among them is high. About one-third of all new businesses fail within one year, half within two. However, if megabucks are your objective, apart from inheritance and marriage, you are almost undoubtedly going to get them as an entrepreneur.

I've observed a number of successful entrepreneurs at close range, and so have others, and they have many interesting similarities. It might be interesting to see some of their characteristics and how they go about building their empires, that is, what makes them tick and how they get a project to fly. Flying may be an appropriate image, for it may not be by chance that a startling number of them have a pilot's license.

For a while, back in the late sixties, making money had a bad vibe attached to it in the minds of many, but it's very much in vogue again. Even young people are coming home to capitalism, provided, of course, it's accomplished with some thought for the well-being of one's associates and without adversely affecting the society as a whole. The new morality is very much in evidence, and there is a bumper crop of under-forty entrepreneur-millionaires out there. They succeed, not as the robber barons and tycoons of our freewheeling past did, but more gently. The new teachings are no longer found in *Fortune* and the *Harvard Business Review* but in *The Whole Earth Catalog* and other New Age journals. Small is beautiful, even, perhaps especially, if it leads to big money. The transitions among this newly emerged and emerging group of entrepreneurs have been manifold and varied: from hedonism to Zen to peace to love to spiritualism to noninvolvement to personal growth to money. Money is OK again, and these new capitalists have "given themselves permission" to acquire it by the long ton.

About one person in every thousand in our society is a millionaire, and the relative proportion is rising. The clearest path to big money is entrepreneurial activity, that is, the founding and running of a business of your own. How do the successful ones go about it?

First, it is clear that even those who are successful have dues to pay. They often spend an apprenticeship period during which they learn how to do whatever it is they intend to do as an entrepreneur. This may sound obvious but lack of adequate experience is one of the major reasons new businesses cannot find financing. Consider a man or woman who has gone through twelve years of primary and secondary school education, four years of college, and four or five years of medical school. Even if such a person were graduated with honors from the best schools in the country, would you want him or her to perform a delicate surgical operation on you? This potentially talented surgeon would normally be expected to be brought along into the profession gradually. By watching and assisting (in minor aspects) practicing surgeons and by slowly accumulating actual on-the-job training and experience, such a person would, in time, become ready to assume a major role in surgical operation. Similarly, would-be pilots must acquire sufficient actual experience under the direction and control of a licensed individual before they are permitted to solo.

Often overlooked by hopeful entrepreneurs in setting up a new business is the fact that an excellent comptroller or production person may not have all of the necessary know-hows to operate a successful business enterprise. Experts in narrow specialties do not have a good track record of success as entrepreneurs.

A friend of mine (who happens to be a licensed pilot) was in charge of a successful copper wire company for several years. The company made millions of dollars of profits, but the parent company siphoned them off and its management began to make the operation of the wire company difficult. My friend, who was extremely capable and experienced, decided to start his own business. With some of his own money, some invested by friends, and a bank loan, he commenced operations on a scale about 20 percent of that of the company he'd been operating. His company has been producing at full throttle ever since, and he has expanded it several times.

At this writing, the company has a net worth of about one million dollars. In five years, it will probably be worth more than five million, and it will probably double again before my friend, who owns half of it, sells it to a larger company. Based on my evaluation of my friend's entrepreneurial ability and the potential of what he wanted to do, I made a small investment in his company. Within the foreseeable future, I expect to be receiving annual dividends equal to my total investment, and I'll probably get back twenty times what I put at risk when I sell my interest. And of course, many jobs and products will have been created.

The pattern of this success is instructive. My friend was highly trained (Harvard and M.I.T.) and had a track record of success in the same kind of business he intended to operate. His reputation and character were excellent. He knew the buyers and the suppliers, and he was thoroughly experienced in every aspect of running the business. He was entering an area he knew well, had a sound business plan that was good enough to show to a bank, and he was beginning on a scale much smaller than he had demonstrated he could handle and which allowed for excellent growth. He also, as will be examined later, had certain personality factors that made him likely to succeed. All of his dues had been paid in full, and all of the homework had been done. His success was not being left to chance.

Another friend of mine decided to become involved with seminars or workshops. He was aware of a strong uptrend in continuing education among adults, in personal growth aspirations, and in the marketing of information and communications in the form of group participatory encounters, usually conducted over the course of one or two weekends. He had demonstrated his entrepreneurial capabilities in some successful real estate ventures and was also a professional writer.

Beginning with a handful of writers and would-be writers in his own apartment, he began to experiment with a format for a writer's workshop. He was able to unlock and improve the skills of writers at levels from beginner to seasoned pro. Soon he was conducting occasional weekend seminars and charging small fees, and the response was gratifying.

For two years, he gained experience, tinkered with, and fine-tuned, his format, improved his presentation, and learned what he could at each level of growth before expanding the size and frequency, not to mention the tuition, of his workshops. He is now affiliated with a college, conducts his seminars at hotels, sells them out, and has a waiting list. Corporations have asked him to conduct his workshop for some of their personnel, and he will soon be expanding into other cities.

Here again, this entrepreneur began on a small scale in an area with which he had marketable skills and created a business from scratch that had a great deal of growth potential. He built his business slowly, learned a great deal from each seminar he conducted (actually soliciting feedback from all of the participants), and adjusted the format of the workshop as well as his marketing approaches until he had an effective presentation and a salable service.

Each of these men was highly trained, and both had advanced degrees. However, neither education nor special training has a high correlation with "making things happen" in this context. Recently, I spent half a day with a man I'd met a couple of years earlier. He had founded a small business that involved selling limited editions of lithographs and had built it to the point that he now sells these works of art all over the country by mail order and has almost two million dollars worth of lithographs in his warehouse.

He often buys large portions of editions in wholesale lots and resells them, in effect, at retail. This was a profitable enterprise, and properly selected works of art were also appreciating in value, but the concept was certainly not original. He did, however, introduce a wrinkle into the business which he credits for a large part of his success.

He has one of the lithographs of each of his editions appraised by a senior member of the official society of appraisers of art in this country, recognized by courts and agencies of the federal government as authoritative. Once such an appraised value has been placed on a single work in an edition, all of the signed and numbered works in that edition may be said to be identical in value. Buyers of each lithograph in such an edition are thus assured they are paying a reasonable price without having to pay a substantial part of the purchase price to obtain such an appraisal for themselves. A copy of the appraisal obtained by the dealer is enclosed with each purchase. Its cost, spread over the number of lithographs offered for sale in each edition, might be only a few pennies. This simple but creative element has helped put the dealer well on his way toward becoming a self-made millionaire.

Here's an even more interesting example of self-made success through entrepreneurial ability. A girl dropped out of high school at the age of fourteen and moved to New York City with three hundred dollars she had saved from her babysitting earnings. She found a part-time job with a real estate company at twenty dollars per week. She kept this job for two years, learned bookkeeping, and began to assist in the selling and leasing of properties.

By the time she was eighteen, she began to earn some larger commissions and had saved enough money to lease and sublet some small residential properties in Manhattan. Three years later, she got her real estate license. At the age of thirty, this young entrepreneur controlled eight million dollars worth of real estate, including thirty buildings in New York.

What is special about these people, and can others be taught how to be successful entrepreneurs? David C. McClelland, Professor of Psychology in the Department of Social Relations of Harvard University, and David G. Winter, a Ph.D. in social psychology, coauthored an interesting book,

Motivating Economic Achievement (The Free Press, New York). Their theory that what they call "n Achievement" (which has a high correlation with entrepreneurial activity) can be learned, was field-tested in Washington, D.C., Oklahoma, and India.

According to McClelland and Winter, people with high n Achievement have four characteristic ways of acting, and other people may be taught to act in these ways, the result of which produce economic achievement in entrepreneurial ways. The four modes of action they suggest are common among those whose need to achieve are high are as follows:

First, these people "tend to set moderate goals for themselves and to work harder when the chances of succeeding are only moderately great." The reason postulated for this behavior is that it represents an attempt to maximize their feelings of satisfaction in reaching goals. If the goal is too easy, there would be little satisfaction in achieving it. If the goal is too difficult, it may be completely out of reach.

McClelland and Winter illustrate this point with a training tool based on the game of ringtoss or quoits. Each subject is given three rings made of rope and shown a peg at a distance. The instruction given is to see how many rings he or she can throw over the peg from any distance the subject chooses. The results varied considerably. Some stood so close they could hardly miss; others took up positions so far away from the peg, success was virtually impossible. A few apparently chose points at which their success was likely (but not assured), and adjusted the distance to their success or failure on the previous attempt. This latter group's behavior is typical of people with high n Achievement. Group discussions follow this exercise. The participants explain why they chose to play as they did, why they set goals and adjusted to failure or success as they did.

The second characteristic McClelland and Winter found among those high in n Achievement is that they "prefer work situations in which they can take personal responsibility for the performance necessary to achieve the goal." They have confidence in their own abilities and consider themselves better able to reach their goals then their competitors. They don't like to gamble on situations over which they have no control, and in a similar way, they also don't relish committee decisions. Both of these kinds of activities fail to satisfy their need for personal responsibility in determining the outcome.

The third characteristic of people with high n Achievement is the fact that they like to know how they're doing. McClelland and Winter discuss the significant difference in the feedback received by a boy in middle childhood who builds or makes something and the same child who writes a theme and hands it in to be graded by a teacher. In the first situation, if the boy, for example, properly wires a radio, presumably it will work. The result is directly related to his performance. The grade he receives on the theme, however, contains many more variables than only his performance and is thus much less directly related to his efforts.

People with high n Achievement like to see the direct relation of their efforts to specific, concrete results. They tend to gravitate toward those activities that satisfy this need. While this attracts them to business more than to the professions, they seem to react to money in an interesting way. They don't appear to work harder for more money but tend to consider money as an indication of how successful a person has been in the past, not as a motivating factor.

The fourth characteristic McClelland and Winter found among those with high n Achievement was greater "initiative in researching their environment." These people are apparently more alert to new entrepreneurial opportunities. They try new approaches, they travel more, they seek out alternate means of accomplishing their objectives. They are more active; they take greater initiative in beginning projects and businesses of their own.

Entrepreneurial ability can be developed. In fact, there is a rather new approach to teaching entrepreneurial ability in the School for Entrepreneurs, located in Tarrytown, New York. In relatively concentrated form, it incorporates a number of learning tools and methods developed by Professor McClelland and Dr. Winter, including the ringtoss experiments.

If you are interested in becoming a successful entrepreneur, and there are disadvantages (in terms of almost certainly reducing the amount of time you will be able to spend with family and friends) as well as opportunities, there are concrete steps you may consider. First, you might look for opportunities among your own present business, social, and recreational activities in which to practice "making things happen." For example, I've seen Johnny Carson interview a California teacher a number of times. After chatting briefly with Johnny, the man introduces, in succession, some youngsters who imitate birdcalls. They are always marvelous, and they invariably bring down the house. Johnny, who is great with elderly people and youngsters, obviously enjoys the segment, too.

Think, for a moment, what it took for the teacher to organize his students in this activity, to bring them up to the level of a successful presentation on network television, to get them booked, and to be invited back, again and again. None of this, we may be reasonably certain, has anything to do with the specifics of this teacher's job. He could be an excellent teacher without engaging in this activity at all. However, he was able to create something on his own and to make it work. He presumably visualized the project, set his goals so that he could take moderate risks, took personal responsibility for the success or failure of the project, got concrete feedback as to how well the project was developing, and showed great initiative in researching the environment and going about doing whatever it took to get national exposure for the students and himself in a format that really is a credit to the true meaning of the educational process. The dedication and the individual goal-setting and achievement of the youngsters come through shiningly, and the success of the presentation is not a chance or accidental occurrence. The effort is clear, and so is the spirit behind it.

In short, this man displays all of the characteristics of n

Achievement, and from the unusual (for an entrepreneur) position of a teacher. Speaking of which, it should be noted that Professor McClelland and Dr. Winter are also members of academe but were able to field-test their theories and get the cooperation of a foundation, agencies of governments, businesses, and many individuals in widespread locations and over a long period of time; a considerable achievement.

There is a growing consensus that includes theoretical discourses of ancient philosophers and theologians and modern scientific experimentation, voodoo dolls and architects' plans, self-hypnosis and biofeedback, to the effect that visualizing, or creating detailed mental pictures of a desired result (good or bad), tends to produce the result visualized. Many recent experiments have involved performance in sports. In one such experiment, basketball players of a given level of skill were divided into three groups. One group was instructed not to practice at all. The second group was given the usual practice periods with emphasis on foul-shooting. The third group was told not to practice but to visualize themselves taking and making foul shots mentally. They were then tested for foul-shooting ability. The second and third group's performances were not different to any statistically significant degree, whereas the performance of the first group was relatively poor. Merely creating the mental picture of succeeding at the given task improved the performance of the task.

This has been demonstrated repeatedly. Recently, a student swam about Manhattan Island and broke Diana Nyad's record in so doing. After the marathon swim, he told reporters he had "seen himself" accomplishing that result time and again. Arnold Schwarzenegger, at the age of fifteen, decided to become a world champion body builder. He repeatedly visualized himself in great detail stepping on stage and winning the title of Mr. Universe. Five years later, he accomplished precisely what he'd visualized. Another champion Arnold, Arnold Palmer, as a youngster used to practice his golf game alone and announce each stroke aloud as if he were a tournament-winning champion being described by a sports commentator on national television. The success he visualized for himself became actualized for him over and over again.

You've probably seen and heard dozens of actors and actresses tell interviewers that they'd *always* wanted to act. In early childhood, they would act out all the parts of a play or movie they'd seen, sometimes improvising costumes and scenery as well. They had visualized themselves on stage again and again. As they grew and developed, they began to take action that would move them toward the realization of their vision.

The detailed mental pictures we give ourselves, coupled with the initiation of action toward these goals, undoubtedly creates a momentum toward their accomplishment. In writing books, for example, I found that if I put a blank piece of paper into the typewriter and began the first line of the page, a need was developed within me to complete the page, whereas if there were no page in the typewriter, this urge was diminished and a great deal more time elapsed without getting on with the project. Dr. Roberto Assagioli has asserted what he calls "the fundamental law that every image has a motor-tendency" and that "visualization is a necessary stage for action."

However, it must be pointed out that merely completing a task or accomplishing a goal or meeting a deadline, in and of itself, does not imply entrepreneurial ability or n Achievement. In demonstrating entrepreneurial ability, there is an important element present that tends not simply to do something, but to satisfy a need for doing whatever it is successfully. That is, the mere completion of a project is insufficient to satisfy the conditions required to constitute entrepreneurial ability. That ability requires doing it better or doing more of it or doing it differently, so that the doing of it produces a successful accomplishment over and above simply completing the project. If "more" happens to be considered "less," the principle remains the same. The person with entrepreneurial ability coming from that point of view would simply do more "less."

Even if this or that reader is not particularly interested in becoming an entrepreneur, it may nevertheless be useful to be able to identify the potentially successful entrepreneur. By becoming aware of the factors that make for success and failure in entrepreneurial acitvity, one may improve his or her chances to profit by making better informed investment decisions. I have used the criteria set forth in this chapter to advantage by not investing money with entrepreneurs too timid or too insecure to take much risk at all and also passed up opportunities to back individuals prone to taking foolhardy risks.

In deciding to invest some money in my friend's copper company, a start-up operation with high odds against success, I took many of the factors discussed above into account. Not only is this individual a moderate risk taker, but there were two other factors that made him a good bet to successfully run his own company. His need for power, for manipulating and controlling other people and situations, is not particularly high and is certainly subordinate to his need for achievement. Those with high power needs often become embroiled in activities counterproductive to the profitability of a business enterprise. Such people like to knock heads with others, to confront, to slug it out toe to toe. Their need to make themselves right and others wrong is not well suited to maximizing profits. Those who don't have such needs are in a better position to get the job done without getting bogged down in side-action clashes.

Similarly, his need for affiliation, although another basic need, is subordinate to his need for achievement. Those with especially high affiliation needs have to be thought well of by all and sundry. They must feel a part of, associate with, and have a sense of belonging, which often clouds their business judgments. Personnel often tend to underperform for these people without fear of dismissal or replacement. Profit margins tend to plummet.

These judgments of personality are subjective and are by no means an expression of how people should or should not behave. They are meant to describe what makes for success in entrepreneurial activity in our society at the present time. People with high power or affiliation needs make valuable contributions, but it may well be that they are better suited to other than entrepreneurial pursuits.

The risks for people who found their own businesses are great, but there are several sweeteners. Private pension and profit-sharing plans can shelter up to 25 percent of their personal income from all taxes, and all increments on these sums are also tax-free until the funds begin to be paid out at retirement. Deferred compensation may be placed into a program guaranteed by an insurance company in a way that compounds gains on (in effect) tax-free dollars, until retirement. Substantial salaries, expense accounts, and other perks are also available to successful entrepreneurs, plus, for some, the joys of doing it "their way" and making it work.

If you walk, just walk.
If you sit, just sit;
but whatever you do, don't wabble.

Unmon

Calling Your Own Plays; Playing Your Own Calls

Steward Emery, cofounder of Actualizations, describes an airline flight to Hawaii, during which the captain invited him up to the flight deck and showed him a piece of sophisticated electronic gear, a relatively new internal guidance system. The on-board system was designed to indicate where the aircraft was at any given moment and where, according to their flight plan, it should be, with almost zero time delay. By monitoring this information, they could make the indicated adjustments in their course. One of the points of the story is that, despite the fact their flight was "in error" approximately 90 percent of the time, that is, not simultaneously at the precise point in time and space designated or preplotted, by making the corrections suggested by the information they received from the internal guidance system, they would be able to arrive at their destination at almost precisely the moment they were due. Wrong 90 percent of the time but able to reach the precise destination at almost exactly the appointed time!

You can develop the same kind of internal guidance system if you permit yourself to become directly attuned to the data in your environment that are continually being fed back to you. However, the more screens you filter the data through before they reach you, the more of other people's psyches they must come through, the less direct your contact is with the reality itself, the less accurate and real and direct and immediate will be your experience of the event and, by extension, of your world. In short, the more you remove yourself from direct contact with life, with reality, the more vague and imprecise and inappropriate your reactions are likely to be and the more out of harmony with "the way things are" your life is likely to become.

Although we all share many basic similarities as human beings, there are, nevertheless, myriad combinations of individual differences. Not surprisingly, therefore, reasonable people, even when they are in your corner or are disinterested, often differ. Furthermore, not all people are reasonable, not all reasonable people always act reasonably, and people who are in your corner or who are disinterested may be in rather short supply when you need them most. Your interests and those of other people are rarely congruent for more than brief periods and may actually be opposed, if only partially. It is therefore important that somebody else's subjective view of a situation not be substituted routinely for your own direct, immediate, firsthand evaluation.

To cite a simple example, suppose you were to ask of somebody who has recently come indoors: "How's the weather?" The subjective response to that question, composed as it is of several variables (personality factors, sex, age, mental state, state of health, amount and type of clothing worn, length of time spent outdoors, what and when the individual ate last, etc.), may hardly be expected to provide reliable advice for you even in this mundane illustration. Even if the comments you received were a useful indicator of a past set of circumstances, they might have little or no value as a guide to your future conduct, as all of the factors that are part of the weather (temperature, barometric pressure, wind velocity and direction, precipitation, etc.) change, sometimes rapidly.

Not only does asking somebody else this sort of question provide a faulty basis for your actions, but it also deprives you of an opportunity to make your own decisions and to develop your own point of view from the experience. The local weather bureau, only a telephone call away, may at least be expected to provide some objective data for you (if you think you need outside help) plus a (less reliable) forecast. By interpreting the data, you gain a firsthand knowledge of how you feel under certain conditions. Dealing with somebody else's opinion or estimate, or other vague shadows on the cave wells, prevents you from playing your own calls. Ralph Waldo Emerson put it this way: "A man should learn to detect and watch that gleam of light which flashes across his mind from within, more than the lustre of the firmament of bards and sages. Yet he dismisses without notice his thought, because it is his."

The reason I labor this point is that I am convinced it will enhance your life, perhaps even save it as it may have saved mine, and the opinions I got were not from people who came in out of the rain but from paid professional experts, the best I could find in New York. In 1964, it was discovered during a routine physical examination that I had a single node growing out of a side of my thyroid gland. Although unlikely, there was a possibility the growth might be malignant. I sought additional opinions.

All of the surgeons I consulted suggested surgery and all estimated the size of the node on the high side. The other specialists also viewed the case through their own respective lenses. As there was such a diversity of opinion, I began to study the literature in the best medical library in the city so that I could participate more intelligently in the decision-making process.

The chief thyroid therapist of a leading New York hospital, a specialist in the field for more than thirty years, did a thyroid scan and uptake, both of which appeared normal to him (and to me). On his recommendation, I took two grains of thyroid hormone daily for a year. At the end of that period, another scan and uptake were done. We were trying to determine what effects, if any, the hormone might have on the node.

The doctor's opinion was that the tests indicated the node to be benign. However, by this time, I had done a great deal of well-motivated research. I disagreed with the doctor's opinion. I told him there appeared to be minor changes in the second scan and the uptake was on the low side. Taken together, it seemed to me surgery was indicated. I asked the doctor to compare the two scans side by side. He went into his study, retrieved the earlier scan, and compared them carefully. After a long silence, he agreed that surgery was indicated. The node turned out to be malignant.

In order to gain your own perspective, you must take the responsibility for your own life. Nobody else should have that responsibility—not experts, not well-intentioned friends or relatives or anybody else. Don't "let George do it" for you. It's your life; you have to "do it" if it is to work for you. The Zen master Unmon is quoted as telling the monks: "If you walk, just walk. If you sit, just sit; but whatever you do, don't wabble." Contrast this approach with that of a man I knew who, while attempting to select some ties at a haberdashery shop one afternoon, scooped up a handful and took them out into the street. "Which of these ties," he asked startled passersby, "go best with my personality?"

If you filter the perceptions you receive through mediators, you deprive yourself of a direct encounter with the event itself. The more you come to depend on the perceptions and opinions of others, the less of yourself are you able to put into the equations of the various experiences of your own life. Soon, if the process continues, your life becomes dim and pale and you are eventually at sea, tossed and buffeted, alone under a starless sky, without an internal compass of your own.

This process of disorientation and dissatisfaction feeds on, and is nourished by, itself. Direct sensory deprivation distorts perceptions. The person with distorted perceptions finds him- or herself less able to cope. A noticeable "wabble" is introduced into his or her life. A feeling of continually being one-down leads to a greater dependence on guidance from others. The guidance is fallible. When it fails, more guides are sought, often even more removed from the reality of the individual's life situation than the former guides. The new guides also fail, often to the accompaniment of rancor and recrimination. A retreat into fantasy and inactivity intensifies the flight from reality. The "wabble" becomes even more pronounced.

You can get behind the wheel of your own life. You can reclaim the controls you relinquished and steer your life in any direction you choose. However, good intentions, positive thoughts, and concrete plans, valuable as they may be, require action if they are to be of any service to you. Acting on your own perceptions of reality and moving toward your goals is an exhilarating and rewarding way of life. The emphasis must be on action; perceptions alone won't get you there. As Emerson put it with grand simplicity: "There is a time in every man's education when he arrives at the conviction that envy is ignorance; that imitation is suicide; that he must take himself for better or worse as his portion; that though the wide universe is full of good, no kernel of nourishing corn can come to him but through his toil bestowed on that plot of ground which is given to him to till. The power which resides in him is new in nature, and none but he knows what that is which he can do, nor does he know until he has tried."

Once you begin to move toward your objectives, your own internal guidance system will clack into action. If you learn to listen, you will discover what works for you and what doesn't, in terms of getting you closer to where you want to be. Your built-in "Geiger counter" will tell you when you are getting warm and when you are moving away from your goals. You may then take corrective action. Like the airliner that was off course 90 percent of the time but arrived at its destination at almost precisely the scheduled time, you will become aware of when to accelerate, when to slow the pace, when to change direction and how to move over and around obstacles.

If you have the will, the way will be open to you. Victor Hugo's familiar line "Greater than the tread of mighty armies is an idea whose time has come" is unexceptionable, but when, precisely, is that time and what caused that particular time to be the proper moment? The answer lies in a continuity of effort. Ideas often take years, sometimes centuries, of effort before their times come. Like a cauldron of water that suddenly begins to boil, the seemingly instantaneous result springs into being only after the expenditure of a great deal of energy.

The so-called overnight success in show business that actually took many years of dedicated work and a long, uphill struggle—interspersed with odd jobs, disappointments, rejections, and failures—is a familiar story. In the same way, there is not a single champion athlete who didn't have to train long and hard for his or her success. Many conquered long odds in the process. Glenn Cunningham, so badly burned in a schoolhouse fire when he was eight that doctors said he would never be able to walk, went on to become the world recordholder for the mile. Wilma Rudolph overcame a serious physical handicap, became a track star, and later won Olympic gold medals.

Although nobody simply jumps into the water and swims the English Channel, the training for the accomplishment of such a feat may begin with the swimming of a single width of a pool, or of one or two strokes, or even with only the concept of being able to do it. At first, the efforts may seem unrewarded and progress may be slow. Soon, however, with continued effort and the adjustments suggested by the direct contact with the obstacles to be overcome, remarkable breakthroughs are achieved.

As the opening of a lock requires the lining up of every tumbler, so does the achievement of any important goal require the surmounting of every impediment that stands between you and your objective. Partial solutions will not suffice. If you fail to line up a single tumbler, the lock will remain closed to you. In the same way, even a single obstacle may effectively block your path. However, with purposeful effort over time, extraordinary results have repeatedly been produced. Sometimes, the outcomes have been unexpected.

Christopher Columbus sought a route to India by sailing west. He reached San Salvador, which he thought was part of eastern Asia, and kept on going. The rest, as the saying goes, is history. The determination of Columbus may perhaps be gauged by the fact that he set out on this journey eighteen years after he conceived the plan and, to underscore the point, here is a line from his log of that voyage: "This day, despite imminent threats of mutiny and storms, *we sailed West because it was our course.*"

"If our young men miscarry in their first enterprises," wrote Emerson, "they lose all heart. If the young merchant fails, men say he is *ruined*. If the finest genius studies at one of our colleges, and is not installed in an office within one year afterward in the cities or suburbs of Boston or New York, it seems to his friends and to himself that he is right in being disheartened, and in complaining the rest of his life. A sturdy lad from New Hampshire or Vermont, who in turn tries all the professions, who teams it, farms it, peddles, keeps a school, preaches, edits a newspaper, goes to Congress, buys a township, and so forth, in successive years, and always, like a cat, falls on his feet, is worth a hundred of these city dolls."

The message is abundantly clear: Hang in, keep the faith, keep going and you'll get there. One of the veteran Broadway showmen likes to say that if an actor manages to survive long enough, they'll build a theater around him. Too many people will believe in almost anything but themselves. The kind of stamina that enables you to stay the course requires a belief in yourself and a willingness to work toward your goals.

Dr. John Lilly reaches the following conclusion: "In the province of the mind, what one believes to be true is true, or becomes true.... In the mind, there are no limits." This may explain the ability of a one hundred ten pound woman, galvanized into action by the sight of a loved one being crushed to death under the weight of an automobile, to rush to the site, raise the car, and permit the victim to crawl to safety.

There are almost innumerable examples of people who have overcome formidable obstacles and achieved their goals by visualizing what they wanted, moving toward their objectives, learning from their experiences, adjusting, and moving forward. If world champion athletes, show business superstars, business, social and political leaders, artists, inventors and creators of every description require time and effort and stamina in order to reach their objectives, isn't it reasonable to assume you will need time and effort and stamina if you are to reach your objectives? Isn't it unrealistic to expect instantaneous results? Waiver, falter, quit, and you remove yourself from the ranks of the eligible. There are no limitations on your successes except those you impose on yourself.

The tendency to "let George do it" is extremely pervasive, and it operates on many levels. We have all heard, for example that to give another a fish only temporarily eases hunger, whereas teaching a person to fish provides a means of satisfying hunger permanently. This concept has important applications to our own daily lives, for how many of us know "how to fish" in a welter of close-to-home waters? Have we come to rely too much on others? Do we require plumbers or building superintendents to handle simple jobs like the changing of a washer? Could we, if left alone for a week, even prepare our regular diet for ourselves? Dependences such as these tend to be carried over into other areas of your life. If you find that you have become overly dependent on others, have you accepted this condition or are you willing to learn and develop and grow?

Only after we are able to meet life directly, to call our own plays and play our own calls, are we able to take the next step beyond mere data and facts. These are items of value, to be sure, but they are of considerably less importance than organizing or underlying principles. The latter explain and predict and enable those who are aware of them to create new and original combinations and theories with greater facility and understanding. Bits and pieces can thus be related to form an integrated whole. The bigger the pieces of reality the principles and theories illuminate, the more useful they are. Our educational institutions place great emphasis on the accumulation of facts and data at the expense of underexposing those who would learn with the more basic and useful building blocks, namely, principles and theories. The possession of the former without the illumination of the latter provides treacherous footing. It leaves those so "educated" in about the position of the natives on a remote Pacific island who, well supplied by U.S. aircraft during World War II, have deified the rusting remains of abandoned aircraft and wait expectantly for their return, as they have for decades. How many of us believe in the same kind of magic?

Taking responsibility for the direction of your life involves making choices and produces a heightened sense of the consequences of your actions. Like the airliner's internal guidance system, your own biocomputers become better attuned to reality by observing the correspondences between your efforts in a given direction and the results achieved. This information is directly and immediately available to you without any of the qualifications, dilutions, or distortions of mediators. Once it is clear that making excuses for yourself or blaming others for this or that lack of success is fruitless and unproductive, your thoughts and energies may be more appropriately utilized in correcting and adjusting and creating the next play. It is important to become free of the fear of failure. Errors are to be expected, and progress may be measured not by a reduction in the number of mistakes you make, but by a reduction in the number of times you repeat the same error.

The general approach suggested in these pages has been working for centuries. You select your own goals and objectives. You make choices; you are able not only to react, but also to act, to take action. You formulate your own plans and take full responsibility for carrying them out. Instead of merely being carried along in the wake of outside forces or drifting aimlessly with the currents, alternately becalmed or tossed by storms, you set your own sails and tack this way and that, toward your destinations. Your senses become sharper and more attuned to the flow of events within your ken. There is a growing sense of harmony between you and the realities of your environment. Like a tuning fork that picks up unseen frequencies and soon begins to resonate with them, you are able to interact in sympathy with the universe from a clear, uncluttered, true perspective.

Once you have wholeheartedly taken the helm of your own life, you can begin to move toward your objectives. Vague, ill-defined goals are obviously much more difficult to achieve than those that are specific and detailed. The details and fine strokes provide clearer landmarks. They create sharp mental pictures and reference points so that your unconscious mind may more easily grasp them and focus on them. It is helpful to write out your objectives in detail and place a time limit on their realization. Committing these desires to paper gives them a concrete, physical, tangible presence and provides additional material for your internal biocomputers to process.

As we have seen, a passive approach to the living of your life removes you from a position of direction and control and places you in the hands of such unreliable factors as chance, luck, and magic. On the other hand, once you learn to produce movement by your own actions, it will become relatively easy to change speed and direction. The activity you generate will provide a channel for personal growth and development. In turn, this will multiply your opportunities for successes, the achievement of goals, and the further enhancement and enrichment of your life. Your activity will create a personal power plant for the creation of opportunities. Inactivity, passivity are unprinted tickets on a disused railroad; they lead to nowhere but stagnation and decay.

Once the conscious and subconscious aspects of your mind become animated by the fact that you can be a cause of what happens in your life, instead of merely an effect, you tend to look for and develop opportunities that will allow your efforts to make a difference. "He who refuses to embrace a unique opportunity," wrote William James, "loses the prize as surely as if he tried and failed." These self-disqualifications will tend to diminish in number and disappear. Your increased self-esteem will make it easier for you to interact with other people and more likely that you do so. At the same time, your growing confidence in your own ability to be a causative agent in your own life will encourage you to express your own creativity and humanity.

The need to react defensively, to express hostility or negativity, or to overreact will disappear, and you will be able to relate to other people and to situations naturally, openly, and wholeheartedly. Your every act and expression will take on the complete authenticity of your being, of your personal identity, and others will be encouraged thereby to relate to you in the same way. As an autonomous individual able to act, able to effect changes, you will tend to take a greater interest in all of the elements in your environment. You will be able to listen more actively and intently to others, and you will be less likely to simply acquiesce passively or pretend to ignore what is being said if you are of another mind.

Your productivity will rise dramatically. You will become more efficient and more purposeful, and you will be able to accomplish more in a given day and in less time. You will be able to take the first step, make the first move, without fear of rejection or failure. You will be able to go the extra distance to make a given opportunity succeed. Success will breed success, and you will gain momentum. The "training effect" of this growth will bring you benefits every day of your life. It is well established that a person's physical condition can be improved by applying loads in gradually increasing amounts. By the same token, the failure to use bone or muscle will cause it to atrophy and die. I am suggesting that the soul and the spirit and one's character also conform to this natural law. Successive overloads will produce remarkable strength, fitness, and resiliency—spiritually as well as physically.

"Eventually," writes Rollo May, "only to the extent to which he grasps reality, can he make this world *his*; if he lives in illusions, he never changes the conditions which necessitate these illusions." Our very identity is a by-product of the living of our lives. Life becomes the great teacher, and those who choose to live their lives once removed, as it were, from direct contact with life, thereby accept for themselves the synthetic and lose that which is most precious—the beauty and the reality of their own persona. That which is truly ours becomes so not by mouthing doctrines handed down to us by others, not by purchase, not by inheritance, not by imitation, but only by "grasping reality." The other avenues lead only to disintegration, that is, a separation from others and from ourselves. In Rollo May's view, mental health is characterized by "... a sense of identity based on one's experience of self as the subject and agent of one's powers, by the grasp of reality inside and outside of ourselves..."

When you have finally knit yourself into an integrated, functioning human being, when you have sealed off the frenzy and the din from without and healed the divisions within, every activity can be a joyful celebration. Preparing a meal, taking a walk, closing a big deal, creating a work of art, or chatting with friends or family—whatever you are about becomes sublimely colored and clothed by the truth and beauty you bring to it.

There is only one person who can prevent you from doing and being your best, regardless of the circumstances. When the connection is made between how much of yourself you are willing and able to put into any particular aspect of your life and how well you do and feel, the message and the method are clear. In putting your best out there in the world, however, don't insist upon an immediate, one-to-one correlation between your efforts and the good result you have in mind. To harbor this expectation sets the stage for much unnecessary frustration and disappointment. In a complex universe, cause and effect cannot realistically be expected to echo one another quite so quickly. A seed requires time in order to germinate, but plant it in fertile soil and tend it faithfully and it will burst through even solid rock, if necessary, to fulfill its destiny.

Your character and positive mental attitude, powered by your own efforts, set a chain of events in motion. This is the direct route, the fast track. As Emerson put it almost a century and a half ago: "So use all that is called Fortune. Most men gamble with her, and gain all, and lose all, as her wheel rolls. But do thou leave as unlawful these winnings, and deal with Cause and Effect, the chancellors of God. In the Will work and acquire, and thou hast chained the wheel of Chance, and shalt sit hereafter out of fear from her rotations. A political victory, a rise of rents, the recovery of your sick, or the return of your absent friend, or some other favorable event, raises your spirits, and you think good days are preparing for you. Do not believe it. Nothing can bring you peace but yourself. Nothing can bring you peace but the triumph of principles."

> **I say that you ought to get rich,**
> **and it is your duty to get rich.**
>
> Russell H. Conwell

Bread:
The Big Loaf

It probably won't come as much of a surprise that the two major objectives in connection with wealth are getting it and keeping it. These two objectives have long been held by purveyors of conventional wisdom to be in essential conflict. Keeping wealth required a low degree of risk of principal, and a low return was associated with low risk. The acquisition of wealth required, at a minimum, "prudent" or "businessperson's" risk, an obviously higher degree of risk than was considered warranted for those wishing only to preserve their capital. Those willing to speculate were permitted to take higher risks in order to chance higher returns.

People steeped in such wisdom pointed to the "pure" interest rate as the price paid for the use of money, a rental charge, as it were, paid by banks for the use of cash and on which there was little or no risk of loss of principal. If a greater return on one's funds were sought, one had to be willing, so it was repeatedly said, to accept correspondingly greater risks. This was a tidy theory and a convenient one, especially for those who brokered, counseled, or otherwise profited from the transactions, as any losses experienced by the advised were more easily passed off and accepted as punishment for greed than as the result of bad advice, and the wheels of the investment world were, with occasional brief times out for oiling and mechanical malfunction, kept turning.

With great respect for its age, if less for its wisdom, I think there are exceptions to, and gaping holes in, the theory. There are, in my view, opportunities for the nimble and knowledgeable to glean large profits accompanied by small potential losses. I have participated in such opportunities and so have many others.

For example, in 1971, when the price of silver bullion was approximately $1.30 per ounce, bags containing a face amount of $1,000 in United States dimes, quarters, and half-dollars minted prior to 1965 and made of coinage metal with a 90 percent silver content, were selling in the marketplace at a price of less than $1,100 each. Regardless of how low the price of silver bullion might have dropped, each bag would always be worth at least its face amount of $1,000. The maximum potential loss on such a purchase was therefore $100 per bag, or approximately 9 percent of the $1,100 commitment (plus a tiny storage and insurance charge).

Each bag contained approximately 720 ounces of silver bullion. If the price of silver bullion were to rise, the price of each bag would also rise. At a price of four dollars per ounce, for example, the silver content alone would be worth $2,880 per bag. In fact, the price of silver bullion rocketed to more than seven dollars per ounce, as each bag of coins more than quadrupled in price.

This is one example of a situation in which a relatively small risk of loss and a high profit potential were available in the same commitment. In addition, this investment offered those willing to raise the ante the factor of leverage. Leverage permits a relatively small amount of invested funds to control a much larger total investment. Relatively minor fluctuations in the value of the property thus controlled will produce a more dramatic impact on the sum invested. In this example, as each bag of coins was money itself, it was excellent collateral for a loan. The entire face amount of the coins could be borrowed so that only the premium, the amount of the cost above the face value (in this example, $100), plus interest on the loaned amount, was required. In the example cited, this leverage factor would have multiplied each $100 thus invested by a factor of 34 (minus interest, storage, and insurance charges).

Silver bullion futures, trading on both the Chicago Board of Trade and Commodity Exchange, Inc., and silver coin futures, trading on the New York Mercantile Exchange, offered additional opportunities to lever an investment in silver. In addition, futures trading would eliminate the interest, storage, and insurance charges but add a relatively small commission. You might have made your investment in silver coin or bullion futures contracts with relatively distant expiration dates, and if you desired to remain in the commitment after the expiration dates, you might have sold the original investment and bought an equal (or lesser or greater) number of contracts in what was then a relatively distant expiration date. Of course, long-term capital gains treatment would require a minimum holding period for each investment, and this would not be so readily available with the "rolled over" commodity futures contracts, as each time you took a new position, a new long-term capital gains period would be recommenced.

At any rate, the tax treatment of gains is not my primary purpose in this context, although later in this chapter I will outline a method for putting off the payment of taxes on capital gains and for converting short-term to long-term capital gains.

In October and December of 1971, I averaged $1.402 per ounce (not the precise bottom, but close enough) on a position of 34,992 ounces of silver bullion. This was an approximately fifty thousand dollar commitment that I bought on 25 percent margin and kept stored in a Swiss bank. I also made several commitments in silver coin futures and silver bullion futures at about the same time, all of which were highly profitable.

Under certain circumstances, the listed stock options markets offer the possibility of high profit/low risk situations. A few years ago, I took fifty-one consecutive profits in the listed stock options markets, evolved and formulated a complex method of trading, and wrote a book on the subject, all within the contractually allotted six-month period.

One trade involved the purchase of 100 shares of stock at $28 per share and the sale of two listed stock options in the same stock at a price of $400 per option. The options were calls, and they gave the buyer the right to pay $30 per share for 200 shares of the stock until their expiration four months later. At the time I made that commitment, *Bought 100 XYZ 28; Sold 2 XYZ April 30 calls 4,* the margin requirement was $1,250, ignoring commissions. That position would have shown a profit (again, ignoring commissions) if the stock were selling at any price between $20 and $40 per share when the options expired four months later, a prospect I considered extremely likely. There might also be numerous additional opportunities to profit prior to the expiration of the options.

In fact, I reversed the entire position twelve calendar days later (I was not seeking maximum profits but to document, if I could fifty-one consecutive profits within six months) for a net, including commissions, of $162 on the $1,250 commitment, a 12.96 percent gain in less than two weeks, about 75 times bank interest. For the sake of completeness, I should add that in order to sell options, a margin account was necessary and there was a requirement of an equity in the account of $2,000 in order to be permitted to trade on margin. Thus, I would not have been allowed to make this commitment with only $1,250. However, as I had other holdings in the account, this position, in fact, required only $1,250 of my funds.

The point is that on December 27, 1974, with four months and one day until the calls expired, I could make this commitment (the stock was Avon Products) with the knowledge that the maximum potential profit was $1,000 and the profit zone was between a price of $20 and $40 for the common stock. This profit zone gave me 8 points of protection on the downside (28.57 percent of the price of the stock) and 12 points of protection on the upside (42.86 percent).

The ratio of shares of stock purchased to the number of calls sold may be altered to fit your pocketbook and your opinion as to whether you need greater protection on the upside or the downside of the stock. The higher the ratio of calls sold to the number of hundreds of shares of stock bought, the more vulnerable you are to maintenance margin calls if and as the stock rises. Brokers will be able to give those interested current details in this regard, the rules of the exchanges, and those of a particular brokerage house. Your opinion as to whether you need more protection above or below the price of the stock is relevant because it is possible to give yourself upside protection for all prices of the stock up to infinity and downside protection to a price of zero for the stock, but not both at the same time. As nature's abhorrence of free lunches is almost as great as it is of a vacuum, the decision as to how many calls to sell in relation to how much stock to buy is pivotal. This ratio determines the maximum profit potential, the margin requirements, and the exposure to risk. This ratio may be adjusted to some extent after the position is taken, but it is best to form your opinion before you take the position. If you wish, you may fine-tune the ratio by selling one call and buying an odd lot (less than 100 shares) of the stock.

In this type of hedge, when the number of hundreds of shares of stock equals the number of calls sold, **Bought 100 XYZ 47; Sold 1 XYZ October 50 call option 7,** and the excercise price of the call option ($50 per share) is above the price paid for the stock ($47 per share), you would be protected against maintenance margin calls up to a price of infinity for the stock, and no matter how high the stock rose in price, your risk of loss would be eliminated. For example, if the stock went to $70 per share, the buyer of the call would exercise his or her right to buy your 100 shares of stock at a price of $50. You would thus have a gross profit on the stock of $300 plus the $700 you received when you sold the call. Your gross profit would be $1,000. This is the maximum profit potential for this hedge, and it would be realized for all prices of the stock above $50 per share at the time the call you sold was exercised.

On the downside, you are protected to the extent the amount you received for the call you sold covers your losses on the stock you bought, ignoring commissions. In this example, you would be protected down to a price of $40 for the stock (or slightly less than 15 percent of the $47 you paid) by the $700 you received for the call.

There may also be opportunities to reverse the entire position at a satisfactory profit prior to the expiration or exercise of the call. In addition, if the stock remains under the exercise price of $50 per share, with the passage of time, the price of the call you sold will decline and you may buy it in at a profit and, if you wish, look for another opportunity to repeat the process by selling another call with a more distant expiration date. Of course, any dividends paid on the stock are yours, too.

One important caveat: The listed stock options markets are somewhat complex, and the rules are subject to change. If you have any inclination to risk a penny, there is no substitute for your own knowledge and understanding. It is imperative you learn what you are about before making any commitment. When you think you are ready, try out your ideas on paper and check to confirm you are playing by the actual rules that prevail in the real world. If you find you are taking fairly consistent profits on paper, and you are still interested, risk only a small percentage of your capital. Should you take three or four losses, and you should limit the size of any loss, leave the game, regroup, and try something else.

Marketplaces and other investment media have personalities of their own, and they seem to favor investors whose personalities are compatible with theirs. I was a member of the so-called financial community for about nine years and have seen a great deal of trading. Repeatedly, the identical advice at the same moment to two different people will net one a good profit and the other a thumping loss on the same security.

For example, one day at lunch, a very dear friend and I decided to buy a stock listed on the Pacific Stock Exchange. We each placed an order to buy 400 shares with the same broker at the same moment, and we each paid the same price for our respective 400-share lots on the stock. A few months later, I told my friend of my intention to take my profit that day. He decided to hold his stock. My gross profit was 66⅔ percent. By a lucky accident, I happened to get the exact top eighth on the stock for that period of time.

My friend continued to hold the stock and saw it return to the price we'd originally paid and even somewhat lower. During the course of more than a year, the stock climbed back to the price at which I'd sold and rose less than a point higher, to a new high. At this writing, the stock is about half a point more than we paid and my friend is still holding. He's been in the position for about two years and has missed many other opportunities in the interim.

Edward C. Thorp, a mathematics professor at the University of California at Irvine, developed a system for beating casino blackjack. His book, *Beat the Dealer*, spells out his system in detail and also offers some practical advice. One valuable tidbit from Thorp is that a player should never play more than once against a dealer to whom he or she has already lost and, as a corollary, players should seek out dealers at whose tables they have been winners. The purpose of this suggestion is to minimize the opportunities for card cheats, if any, to beat a player.

Thorp's point can be extended to investment situations, and its application goes beyond cheating. My advice would be that if you suffer three or four consecutive losses with a particular broker or in a particular investment medium, quietly discontinue your involvement, if possible, and try again elsewhere when you are once more ready to play. I take bad results to be an indication that the environment is not propitious. The chemistry or the timing or the vibes or whatever ineffable quality required to make this particular cake rise for you is missing. It's nothing personal, but the clear message that reads out is: Don't press it. Pass and regroup. It is so incredibly easy to make of any bad situation a complete disaster (not only in investments but in any aspect of living) that the avoidance of this trap is of tremendous value. If you suddenly receive bad news or if somebody drops an important ball for you, you may be inclined to crack the whip or otherwise press to make up for lost time or money or some other value of which you feel temporarily bereft. You may feel the need to express rancor or recrimination or to make accusations and fix blame. At precisely that moment, warning lights and alarm bells should be alerting you that you are being presented with a golden opportunity to convert some admittedly unpleasant situation into a full-scale, unmitigated disaster. Limit your loss is the rule. Don't go for broke and don't let the ball play you.

Speaking of rules, one of the great traders in the history of Wall Street was a man named William D. Gann. Back in those freewheeling days during the twenties and early thirties, before the creation of the Securities and Exchange Commission, when buccaneers were even more unbridled than they are today, Gann was patiently and painstakingly studying the stock and commodity markets and pocketing profits. His methods were well ahead of their time, and he amassed, and kept, a great fortune. If memory serves, it was Gann who financially supported the more flamboyant Jesse Livermore (the Boy Plunger) when the latter fell on hard times. In the forward to his book *Truth of the Stock Tape* (which I ferreted out of a used-book store after a long search) written in 1923, Gann speaks to us across the decades: "If I succeed in teaching only a few to leave wild gambling alone and follow the path of conservative speculation and investment, my work will not have been in vain and I will have been amply repaid..."

In another book, *Wall Street Stock Selector*, copyright 1930, Gann sets forth what he calls "Twenty-Four Never-Failing Rules" for making profits in the stock market. He counsels that traders be sure they do not violate any of these rules and that if you take a loss, you go over the rules and discover which you violated so that you don't repeat the error. A half-century later, the rules prove to have been so well stated they bear repetition for the more than thirty million people in this country alone who are in the stock market:

Twenty-Four Never-Failing Rules

1. Amount of capital to use: Divide your capital into 10 equal parts and never risk more than one-tenth of your capital on any one trade.

2. Use stop loss orders. Always protect a trade when you make it with a stop loss order 3 to 5 points away.

3. Never overtrade. This would be violating your capital rule.

4. Never let a profit run into a loss. After you once have a profit of 3 points or more, raise your stop loss order so that you will have no loss of capital.

5. Do not buck the trend. Never buy or sell if you are not sure of the trend according to your charts.

6. When in doubt, get out, and don't get in when in doubt.

7. Trade only in active stocks. Keep out of slow, dead ones.

8. Equal distribution of risk. Trade in 4 or 5 stocks, if possible. Avoid tying up all your capital in any one stock.

9. Never limit your orders or fix a buying or selling price. Trade at the market.

10. Don't close your trades without a good reason. Follow up with a stop loss order to protect your profits.

11. Accumulate a surplus. After you have made a series of successful trades, put some money into surplus account to be used only in emergency or in times of panic.

12. Never buy just to get a dividend.

13. Never average a loss. This is one of the worst mistakes a trader can make.

14. Never get out of the market just because you have lost patience or get into the market because you are anxious from waiting.

15. Avoid taking small profits and big losses.

16. Never cancel a stop loss order after you have placed it at the time you make a trade.

17. Avoid getting in and out of the market too often.

18. Be just as willing to sell short as you are to buy. Let your object be to keep with the trend and make money.

19. Never buy just because the price of a stock is low or sell short just because the price is high.

20. Be careful about pyramiding at the wrong time. Wait until the stock is very active and has crossed Resistance Levels before buying more and until it has broken out of the zone of distribution before selling more.

21. Select the stocks with small volume of shares outstanding to pyramid on the buying side and the ones with the largest volume of stock outstanding to sell short.

22. Never hedge. If you are long of one stock and it starts to go down, do not sell another stock short to hedge it. Get out at the market; take your loss and wait for another opportunity.

23. Never change your position in the market without a good reason. When you make a trade, let it be for some good reason or according to some definite plan; then do not get out without a definite indication of a change in trend.

24. Avoid increasing your trading after a long period of success or a period of profitable trades.

Some additional sage advice comes from another source. The legendary J. P. Morgan, who certainly was not backward when it came to decorating his side of the table with the other players' chips, was once approached by the journalists of the day after the Kruger swindles came to an end with the suicide of Ivar Kruger, the Swedish match king. Kruger had built an empire and controlled, among other business enterprises, about 65 percent of the world's production of matches. In the process, he had defrauded with his complex schemes, not widows and orphans, but heads of government, investment bankers, and other high financiers, to the beguiling melody of about two billion dollars. When asked by the reporters why it was that he, almost alone of the heavy hitters of the financial community, had managed to avoid Ivar's outstretched hands and seductive voice, old J. P. replied to the effect that he followed a simple rule: If he listened to a man for more than five minutes and still could not understand what the man was talking about, he never invested a dime. Sounds about the way Joe Louis put it.

Unfortunately, many people are still being parted from their hard-earned, harder-saved, dollars by flimflam artists, financial advisors who are amateurs in their chosen profession, and vested brokers with vested interests in creating commissions for themselves. On this latter aspect, I think it represents a direct conflict of interest for brokers' incomes to be based on the volume of transactions they generate when they know, or should know, that statistically the more their accounts trade, the better their chances of losing money.

Half-truths and whole cloth have cost millions, billions. The antidote is vigilance and knowledge. Vigilance does not imply closing your mind to new ideas. Such an approach to the possibilities life offers would be self-defeating. Zest and vitality do not thrive under these restrictions and limitations, nor does a thick carapace or a snug cocoon aid in the dance of life.

The kind of vigilance I have in mind implies an understanding of context and subtext. What may reasonably be expected of this new opportunity? What are the risks and the pitfalls? How much might it cost? Is it subject to a further call on your resources of time, energy, money? How did this opportunity arise? If it originated from a source other than yourself, what is your evaluation of this source? Is the source reliable and honest? What is the motivation for enrolling you in the project? Is the source skillful and knowledgeable? What is the track record of the source? What do your instincts tell you about this opportunity? Does it make sense at first blush?

Only if you are satisfied with the answers to all of these preliminary questions should you be willing to investigate the opportunity further. If time won't permit further investigation, either because the opportunity is a "now or never" proposition, or because you're preoccupied with other matters, pass and await future opportunities.

Knowledge, we are told, is power but, we are cautioned, a little learning is a dangerous thing. As all knowledge is incomplete, the question arises in the context of investments, as in many other aspects of living, how much is enough? If you are simply following the advice of somebody else and do not have a basis on which to formulate your own opinion, your knowledge is insufficient to support backing another's judgment. You may, if you wish, point to the advisor's gleaming track record (and how carefully have you actually checked it) and decide to commit your funds on this basis, but in the words of Sam Goldwyn, "Include me out." You may have some extremely astute friends who may occasionally be willing to carry you along for a free ride, but you should prepare yourself to carry your own weight fairly quickly, for you won't be getting any lighter en route.

My personal bias toward joint investment decisions is negative. Investment clubs and the like have never interested me. There is usually not much to be gained from joint buying of securities that cannot be duplicated individually. The responsibility of advising others, the obligation to follow the group's wishes, and the wobbly compromises don't make much investment sense to me.

There are, however, certain opportunities in which a pooling of talent can make an important contribution to the deal. For example, real property may involve a combination of legal, accounting, real estate, electrical, plumbing, carpentry, contracting, financial, management, and other expertise. The size of the individual commitment may be sufficiently large so as to make sharing or pooling of interests and talents a natural and also increase the profitability of the deal. If such an arrangement seems attractive on its own merits and you happen to lack one of the needed skills, it might be possible for you to substitute a contribution of some of your own time and energy to the project while you learn more about owning and operating real property.

It is obviously desirable to shelter your income from taxes. The federal government, in a burst of ratiocination, has created a number of tax loopholes for millions of us to enjoy. The policy behind these tax benefits is to permit more of us to become self-sufficient when we retire. Legal machinery designed to give retired workers a better chance to receive their corporate pensions is finally being put in place. In addition, individual retirement accounts are now available to millions not covered by corporate plans. Best of all, there is an opportunity to set up a professional corporation (if you happen to be one of the professional people included in the legislation) or your own private pension and profit-sharing plans (through a corporation) and place up to 25 percent of the salary the corporation pays you beyond the reach of the tax collectors. These tax-free amounts and whatever increments they achieve through investment and/or savings may not be paid out without penalty until you reach age fifty-nine and a half. It is relatively simple to set up such plans if you are a covered professional, if you are self-employed, or if you are not otherwise covered and can convince the corporation for which you work to do so (and if the tax benefits warrant doing so).

Those with substantial assets and/or those in high tax brackets should also benefit from sound estate planning. A relatively small fee to competent professionals is money well spent if you are in the upper brackets. I suggest you avoid the common practice of fee-splitting (they prefer to call it referral or forwarding fees) among lawyers. In fee-splitting, you are either charged a higher fee by the second lawyer, who does the work—which amount includes the referral fee to the first lawyer for sending you to the second lawyer—or you are charged the going rate by the second lawyer. However, as part of this amount is split with the referring attorney, the lawyer doing the work for you is underpaid, usually resulting in a lack of motivation or priority for you. You may finesse both of these unattractive alternatives by asking a competent doctor with whom you have a good relationship to recommend a good tax person. The doctor is probably in a high enough tax bracket to be able to refer you to somebody competent from his or her own experience. Such a referral, from a professional in one field to a professional in a different field, is done as a professional courtesy and doesn't ordinarily involve fee-splitting. In this way, you may obtain a personal referral to a presumably good professional person and at a fair (unsplit) fee.

There are a number of techniques that may be used to defer taxes on capital gains as well as on ordinary income. In addition, we may be able to convert ordinary income into capital gains. First, it must be emphasized that I am not a tax advisor and even if I were, the tax laws are subject to change as well as to interpretation. It is therefore essential that anybody who would like to accomplish the objectives set forth above consult a competent professional who would be able to make specific recommendations. Ask questions and try to provide yourself with a basis on which to make a decision. Learn as much as you can. Ask for references you may read for yourself. Get a second opinion. If it's all gobbledegook to you, remember old J. P. Morgan's advice.

At this writing, silver futures spreads used for the purpose of postponing short-term capital gains have been disallowed by the Internal Revenue Service, and the case is in the courts. Whether or not this decision is eventually rejected, there are other means available which appear to be promising, particularly if used with good tax advice and competent brokerage.

Ginnie Mae (Government National Mortgage Association) Mortgage Interest Rate Futures trade in contracts of one hundred thousand dollar (face amount) certificates on the Chicago Board of Trade. By taking a position involving the purchase of one expiration date and the sale of an equal amount of a different expiration date, both of which expiration dates are in the following year, you would hope to create a large gain and a large, offsetting loss.

Toward the end of the current year, you would reverse all or part of the trade that would establish your loss and simultaneously reinstate a position similar to the one you closed out, but in a different expiration date. The entire position would be closed out in the following year. This method, presumably, would meet the objective of deferring taxes on capital gains you'd already taken in the current year.

I've noted that the people who do best, whether their game is making and/or keeping money or tiddledywinks, are more often than not reaping the benefits of the best coaching available. They are willing to pay both the fees and the dues to own a sound position or foundation and a game plan based on the real yard goods: knowledge and the know-how to apply it effectively. Like most others, I've spent time and money both wisely and foolishly, but the payments I've made to buy knowledge and the understanding to implement it or to integrate it into my life, have consistently been my best investments, for unless you gain a solid grounding of your own, you are forever putting the steering mechanism of your own life into the hands of another.

There is another device or method you might consider if you wish to reduce taxes by converting short-term gains to long-term gains and/or to defer to a future year taxes on gains you wish to take in the current year. Again, this opportunity, which involves selling call options, should be checked with your own tax advisors to assure it is available and suitable for you at such time as you may want to use it.

Let's say, for example, you own stock on which you have a paper profit that would give rise to a short-term gain if you sold it this year. Next year, when you've held it long enough to qualify for the benefit of long-term capital gains tax treatment, the gain (or part of it) may have disappeared. What can you do to improve your position?

You may sell a call option on the stock (one call option for each 100 shares you own) with an expiration date after the minimum long-term gain holding period of your stock and at an exercise price above the current market price of the stock.

Say you bought 300 shares of XYZ in July at $25 per share. It's late November and the stock is selling at $29 per share. You have a short-term gain. You sell 3 calls on XYZ with an expiration date of June of next year at an exercise price of $30. Let's assume you receive a premium of 2½ ($250 for each call you sell, or a total of $750, minus a commission). The $750, minus commission that you received for the calls you sold is not taxable until the following year unless you decide to close out the calls by buying them back in the marketplace at a profit.

If the calls you sold are exercised and your stock is called, you will receive the exercise price, in this case, $30 per share, and you will keep the premiums you received for the calls you sold in any case. If your stock is called after it becomes eligible for long-term gain tax treatment, you have converted a short-term gain to a long-term gain, earned the premium for the calls, and actually increased your per share profit from $4 to $5.

If the calls are exercised prior to the time you have held the stock long enough to qualify for long-term capital gains treatment, you have a choice. You may accept the short-term gain, which has been increased from $4 to $5 per share, plus the premium for the calls you sold, or you may go into the marketplace and buy as much stock to deliver as shares called, keeping your original position intact. This will produce a short-term loss and reduce your tax in the year you sustain it. You may then sell new options and repeat the procedure.

If the stock falls in price while you have sold the calls but before it qualifies for long-term gain tax treatment, you are fully protected to the extent of the premium you received, in this case, 2½ points (not including the commission), and you have an opportunity to convert a short-term gain to a long-term gain.

The same approach may be used to defer capital gains, long or short-term, which you have not yet taken in a given tax year, to a future tax year.

Spirit

Some months ago, I heard a eulogy in which a line was quoted from the tombstone of Sir Christopher Wren. Best known as an architect, Sir Christopher was also a mathematician and an astronomy professor. During the late seventeenth and early eighteenth centuries, he designed more than fifty London churches, many of which still stand. St. Paul's Cathedral is considered his greatest building, and he is buried in its crypt.

The line quoted was: "If a monument be needed, look about you." It has a haunting quality and, although I heard it on a sad occasion, in it there is a hopeful direction. To generalize the thought, if all of humankind need a monument, all we need do is look about us. In doing so, there seems to be present a new spirit, a new energy, a lightness and a joy abroad in the land, long absent and sorely missed. The Pepsi Generation is switching to carrot and parsley juice, and despite some notable exceptions, the age-old conflict between the forces of life and death is becoming resolved in favor of life. Even many of those not born again have a new sense of aliveness.

When Einstein and Freud met earlier in this century, they agreed that the future of humanity rested on the sentiments of humankind. Much is being done to ensure that the future of which they spoke rests a bit more securely today than when they discussed it. Many have contributed. Some have given their lives. I think Maharishi, for one, has done a great deal in a relatively short time to raise the consciousness of millions of people, and the ripple effect has reached many times that number. There is a prodigious amount of energy being poured into a current project that has as its objective the elimination of hunger in the world before the end of this century. Thousands of people are hard at work cleaning up the spiritual landscape.

There is much work to be done and there are ebbs and flows, but more and more people seem to be getting the message (and passing it on) that the world is a pretty good place in which to live and each of us can make it better. It's a long process, a little like trying to bring a vast body of water back to life, but there comes a time when you know your efforts are gaining on the problem; you have the objective in sight and you've got the momentum. Effort and direction finally create a turning point, a "critical mass," with which to overcome the problem at hand.

"And He's allowed me to go up to the mountain. And I've looked over," said the Rev. Dr. Martin Luther King, Jr., "and I've seen the Promised Land." I believe it. It's out there and others have also sighted it. It's not easy for anybody to take the flat-out position that the world is entering a new Age of Enlightenment in the face of international problems of such major proportions as war, terrorism, starvation, environmental pollution, and others. Yes, the Four Horsemen of the Apocalypse are still alive and well. They're still riding, and their progeny are being trained and equipped. However, like the meaningless dull roar of a crowded stadium whose strands of conversation, when separated, yield intelligible messages, so, too, are certain messages penetrating the consciousness of the world.

"Let the word go forth," said President John F. Kennedy,

"from this time and place, to friend and foe alike, that the torch has been passed to a new generation of Americans—born in this century, tempered by war, disciplined by a cold and bitter peace, proud of our ancient heritage—and unwilling to witness or permit the slow undoing of those human rights to which this nation has always been committed and to which we are committed today." Many of us still believe that. "War no more. No more war," said Pope John XXIII, and the world watched and prayed. "We have a liftoff." "Four hours and twenty-seven minutes into the mission and still counting." "That's one small step for man, one giant leap for mankind." Begin and Sadat hugging one another. "We hold these truths to be self-evident, that all men are created equal; that they are endowed by their Creator with certain unalienable rights; that among these are life, liberty, and the pursuit of happiness."

The chase is on and the gap narrows. The Four Horsemen have built up a long lead, but we have the means to overtake these remorseless riders and dismount them forever if we have the spirit and the will to do so. Why not "War no more"? And if a meaningful proportion of the resources of the universe were diverted, why not no more famine, no more pestilence, and, yes, even no more death?

Is this an impossible dream? Is "a place where no one cries, a land where no one dies" only a land of make-believe? "I have a dream," said the Rev. Dr. Martin Luther King, Jr., and he raised the consciousness of the country and the world. May we not also dream?

The artists of a society continually pick up the vibrations that cross their sensory fields and their intuitions and weave them into their art. Their antennae are sensitively attuned. Often, what they produce is both a barometer and a harbinger. There are wisps and portents from these sources that indicate the presence of a new wave of reconciliation rising in the world. Humanity has been surfeited with people-created death and destruction. The mass media have carried these messages into our homes and minds to the point that we cry out for deliverance. We don't want to see any more mushroom clouds or the distended bellies and vacant stares of starving children.

On the very day this is being written, the thirtieth anniversary of the Universal Declaration of Human Rights, President Carter said: "Human rights is the very soul of our foreign policy." We have a right to expect enlightened leadership from the leadership community of the world. With the stakes as high as they are, we are entitled to demand no less. We in the developed nations have a special responsibility to provide such leadership as the consequences of our actions, good and bad, tend to be far-reaching. The kind of "guidance" provided by a hammer driving a nail into a board is a poor model. Compassionate interaction and the encouragement of excellence may not only be more humane but more effective as well.

With more than one hundred fifty member states in the United Nations, it is clear that the fabric of the global society cannot continue to take the wear and tear of one hundred fifty daily tugs from every direction. Regional blocs of states may emerge to become larger blocks to be fitted into the total pattern of one planet indivisible.

With the world shrunk so small that it comes into your living room and bedroom every day and seeps into your consciousness, there is no longer any place to hide. You and I cannot live happily ever after while millions perish needlessly each day. The words of our forefathers to the effect that we must all hang together or we will surely all hang separately take on even larger significance today. What is required is nothing less than a transformation in our thinking, a peaceful revolution of our minds and consciousnesses, and it is happening all over the world. Pope John XXIII in "Pacem in Terris" said: "It is not fear which should reign but love, a love which tends to express itself in a collaboration that is loyal, manifold in form and productive of many benefits."

It begins with the self. Each of us produces a jumble of communications and influences and by-products in our daily lives. Let's call that jumble your "sound" or your "vibe" or your "music." Many are unaware they have such a characteristic sound, although they can readily distinguish it in others. You can learn to be your own best teacher, and it requires only a little observation and resolve. "Sometimes," as Yogi Berra said, "you can observe a lot just by watching," and, of course he was right.

Become aware of what it is in others that reaches you, that touches you. For example, did you ever watch somebody in person or on television or in film who touched you so deeply you were moved to tears or you felt like standing up and cheering? Somebody who rocked you right out of your seat? You may have been reacting to the honesty, the humanity, the warmth, the courage to open up and be vulnerable, that came through from that person to you. Whatever it was that affected you, are you ready to feel and to express those qualities in your own life? Can you put into your own "music" that which, whatever it may be, moves you in others? If not now, when?

It's so easy to become locked into a routinized pattern that silently drains your life of reality, hollows you, and blunts your very being, as I know from my own personal experience. On the other hand, by a single act of will, you can alter this pattern in favor of life, of vitality, of reality. The truth is at hand at all times but it sometimes requires a great personal effort to see it. Often in this intense struggle we find the way back to ourselves; we become unified with our own nature. Unless this is accomplished, the individual will forever seek to be buttressed from outside of himself or herself, only to be let down by a false prop or a factor not previously taken into account.

The past need not determine the future. To a person who thinks they are holding up the building against which they are leaning (or vice versa), no amount of dissertation will change their mind so long as they continue to lean against the building. It is only when a person finds the strength and the courage to risk standing away from the building that he or she can truly understand it is no longer necessary to cling to it.

For the man or woman who has become enlightened, there are no props, no artificial supports. He or she needs none. Once he or she has seen into the nature of his or her own being . . . such a person may rely on his or her being . . . the self. Such a person has nothing to fear. He or she is truly at home in the world.

In sharp contrast, the ordinary person is in opposition to their world. Such a person is involved in an endless struggle to control or manipulate the various elements of the world with which he or she collides. Apparent successes are always short-lived; the satisfactions thus derived, fleeting. Unless you discover who you are and become unified with your own nature, you face endless alternation between seeking the support of false props and being disappointed or frustrated all too soon. The result is a kind of living death in which your spirit, your creativity, your being itself is blocked and stunted.

There is an increasing awareness that Western philosophy, with its categories, its dichotomies, its dilemmas, its multiplicity of dualisms, has cut humankind off from their own nature. It has fashioned a world of objects to be manipulated by the mind. It has produced a constant state of conflict, of opposition, of disharmony. Humanity has become a combatant in an all-out struggle with the environment. The result has been a perpetual, if nonetheless false, clash of power.

Some people enter into interactions with others that seek to bind the other person, to limit his or her growth to their own. Some seek involvements as a means of avoiding the business of living their own lives. They wish to delegate their lives to another. In either case, whether you become the custodian of another's life and hold it to a standard outside of its own nature on the one hand, or throw your own life into the pot for safekeeping, you are in a situation that is ultimately deadening.

The living truth begins with the individual, the self. From Buddha to Buber, from Basho to the Beatles, we have heard the same message so many times we no longer listen. The languages may have been different, but the meanings are the same. "Know thyself." "To thine own self be true. . . ." "A sound mind in a sound body." "Love thy neighbor." The Golden Rule. The Golden Mean. Balance, beauty, truth, love, peace.

Those who wish to reenter the living of their lives must have the courage to strip away and discard all the layers of what is not truly their own. In that way, they will no longer simply be watching their life being lived from some points outside of it; they will become directly involved with that life, immediately and personally. In so doing, their lives will take on reality, authenticity, enrichment. They will no longer seek to imitate others or aimlessly follow the directions of others. They will be free to be themselves and to enjoy themselves. The enlightened, creative person is simply being himself or herself, being alive, being in life and expressing his or her own uniqueness. Life becomes unbounded, continuous, a process that is never completed.

By thus returning to what is your own irreducible self, you are left with what is undeniably yours, that which nobody can take away from you—namely, your own authenticity, your very identity. As you interact with life from the bedrock of what is completely and totally your own, you are able to enter into living situations according to the nature of your own being. You are free of all of the false elements, the secondhand, the wholesale merchandise, the hand-me-downs you and others had been so ready to fasten onto you. You are free to face life wholeheartedly at last.

The importance of this wholehearted engagement with life can scarcely be overestimated. The world stands delicately balanced, as it has for centuries, between the forces of Eros and Thanatos. A small shift in either direction will be decisive, and this time every vote counts, even those of people who don't vote, who have no opinions, who are undecided, who are out to lunch, or who already gave.

By the time you read this, regular flights of the space shuttle will have been planned, ushering in an era of astounding new potentials. We will have gone, in the whisk of a single generation, from wishing on a star to living and working on stars. We are already probing deep space and have received radio signals from Jupiter, about 400,000,000 miles away. The laser and a new world of photonics will produce a whole series of miracles in energy, communications, medicine, and alchemy, for openers. The human race stands at a new threshold beyond which, if we permit ourselves to cross it, we can produce an abundance for all of us beyond that which anybody who ever lived ever had. All that stands between us and this cosmic Promised Land are, as I view it, the death throes of Thanatos itself.

It is time to choose life over death. It is time to let the dead past bury its dead. Regardless of our particular circumstances, each of us can make a contribution to life and to our own happiness. Each of us has a part to play. Each creates ripple effects and consequences. Each is needed, is wanted, and will be sorely missed if not on the field when the whistle blows. You shall be happy, and it shall be well with you. Keep the faith, and it shall come to pass. Not too long ago, I came close to throwing in the hand. I've seen resignation and fear and desperation in faces in every region of this country (and we're doing relatively well). But the times they are a-changin'.

There is no limit on your growth as a person except that which you impose on yourself, but to redeem this claim you must have the spirit and the will to take the wheel of your own life. No more self-imposed limits, no more self-inflicted wounds.

Life offers many chances, but chances imply risks. The immobilizing fear of making your own mistakes is itself a mistake. Life is not a final examination or a test in a textbook. There are no correct answers in the back of the book. There are no cameras grinding on you, no tape recorders gathering up evidence of your errors to be later used against you. There are no meanings apart from life. Life consists in the living of your life, in making choices. Find your own nature, and do not fear to follow it. Do not shrink from life, and do not be afraid to live.

If you came into this book at the beginning, you may

recall that all I ever really wanted was to be myself, to be at home in the world, and to do well by doing good. At last the wheel is turning, a heavy door is opening for me and admitting the light into my own life. You have the power to re-create your own life the way you want it to be if you have the spirit and the will. The wisest man I know said that good circumstances and bad circumstances are only circumstances. It isn't the so-called breaks, but how you live through the breaks, that determine the outcome. You begin where you find yourself. Your spirit and your will provide the linkage that can put your life in gear and make it soar.

You shall be happy, and it shall be well with you. To which, having begun with the words "Once upon a time...," I would add only...and may you live happily ever after.